FATIMA, RUSSIA
AND
POPE JOHN PAUL II

Pope John Paul II and Sister Lucia at Fatima, May 1991

FATIMA, RUSSIA
AND
POPE JOHN PAUL II

How Mary intervened to deliver Russia
from Marxist atheism
May 13, 1981–December 25, 1991

by

TIMOTHY TINDAL-ROBERTSON

THE RAVENGATE PRESS
Still River

This first American edition is published by agreement
with the publishers of the original edition, Augustine
Publishing Company, Chulmleigh, Devon, England, and
is being co-published by Augustine Publishing Company as a second British edition.

Imprimatur:
+Timothy J. Harrington
Bishop of Worcester
July 29, 1992

The *Imprimatur* is an official declaration that a book or
pamphlet is free of doctrinal and moral error. No impli-
cation is contained therein that the authority granting
the *Imprimatur* agrees with the content, opinions or statements expressed.

ISBN: 0-911218-23-8 (Clothbound)
ISBN: 0-911218-24-6 (Paperbound)

Library of Congress Catalog Card Number 92-82615

Please address orders and inquiries to:
The Ravengate Press
Post Office Box 49
Still River, Massachusetts 0146

PRINTED IN THE UNITED STATES OF AMERICA

CONTENTS

ILLUSTRATIONS

AUTHOR'S
PREFACE

THIS BOOK REPRESENTS A LAYMAN'S ATTEMPT to understand what Pope John Paul II has sought to accomplish for God and the Church, by effecting the consecration of Russia to Mary's Immaculate Heart in March 1984, in fulfillment of the request of Our Lady of Fatima. It has been written to answer the question I have been asking myself, and which people have been asking me: may we now believe that the astonishing events which have been taking place in recent months in the former Soviet Union are attributable to the intervention of the hand of God, through the intercession of the Blessed Virgin Mary, following the Holy Father's consecration? And are they the beginning of the fulfillment of her promise at Fatima, to deliver Russia from atheism, once her requests had been complied with?

What has happened in Central and Eastern Europe has profound implications for the Church as it stands on the verge of the third millennium. If what we have been witnessing is truly the work of God, then it is important for the future that we should understand what God is saying to us through these momentous events. Because of the urgency of the situation, I have not attempted the fuller account which such a thought-provoking subject merits. Instead, I have confined myself to presenting some of the most significant signs, events and testimonies of a supernatural character which taken as a whole, clearly justify an affirmative response to the above questions. It is my sincere hope that readers who have not yet come to this belief will find the evidence in these pages convincing, and that those who do already believe it will find fresh light and confirmation for their convictions.

I have tried to ensure accuracy within the limited resources at my disposal, and I apologize if, unintentionally, I have omitted to seek permission for the use of material from other sources. Upon notification, such errors and omissions will gladly be rectified in a subsequent edition.

I am more grateful than I can say to Dr. Michael O' Carroll, CSSp, for his stimulating Introduction, and to the authorities in the Sanctuary of Fatima for reading and approving the text, and for permitting the book to be sold in the Sanctuary Bookshop.

My heartfelt gratitude goes out to all our kind friends who have given me their valuable assistance and encouragement in writing this work, as well as to those who have generously given me permission to reproduce their own material, which I acknowledge where cited in the text. I particularly wish to thank Fr. Frederick L. Miller, STD, for the two citations that are used with permission from *Soul* magazine, published by World Apostolate of Fatima, Washington, New Jersey, copyright 1991.

This Preface was originally written for the first British edition of this book, published in April. This first American and second British edition has been expanded and enhanced by the addition of important new material that was not available to me before.

In the first place, I gratefully acknowledge the kind assistance of the authorities at Fatima in providing me with many of the photographs printed in this edition, and for giving me permission to reproduce them.

And secondly, the text of this edition contains three additional documents, each of which brings striking new confirmation to the overall theme of this work. As a result of attending the Congress on "Fatima and Peace" in May 1992, I have been able to include at the end of Chapter 3 the inspiring homily which His Eminence Cardinal Jan Korec of Nitra, Slovakia delivered to the Congress on May 10. Next, the complete text of Mikhail Gorbachev's article of March 1992, as well as of the audience in which the Holy Father commented on it to its publishers, *La Stampa*, has taken its place naturally as the fitting conclusion to a re-shaped Chapter 4. Finally, I have added the personal and stirring account of Bishop Hnilica on how he came to consecrate Russia at the same moment as the Holy Father, inside the Kremlin itself, as part of a new Chapter 6.

I dedicate this work to the Immaculate Heart of Mary, and pray that all who come to read it may be led to find in their own lives the consoling reality of Our Lady's words to Lucia in June 1917: "Do not lose heart. I will never forsake you. My Immaculate Heart will be your refuge and the way that will lead you to God."

Timothy Tindal-Robertson
27 May 1992
St. Augustine of Canterbury

INTRODUCTION

by Dr. Michael O'Carroll, CSSp

ON SEPTEMBER 3, 1843, the first missionary bishop to modern Africa, Edward Barron, an Irishman who had worked in Philadelphia, made a remarkable act of faith in the Blessed Virgin Mary. He formally consecrated the vast area in West Africa entrusted to him and to the Society of the Holy Heart of Mary, founded by the Jewish convert, Francis Libermann, to the Immaculate Heart of Mary. Later in the same century, the same formal dedication was made at Bagamoyo in East Africa of the measureless expanse there awaiting evangelization. Today the Catholic Church in Africa, eighty million strong, is the success story of the last half millennium. The reader may compare the statistics with those of other areas evangelized over many centuries; he will also note the solid organization, the flowering of Christianity in every department of life, the manifold characteristic fruits of the Spirit of Christ.

Here is an advance model of what we may hope for in Russia, which is the great theme of Mr. Timothy Tindal-Robertson's highly informative and carefully documented book. I would wish to emphasize some of the points he makes. But first I wholeheartedly agree with his basic assumption: the power and re-source of the Heart of Mary are, beyond all compre-hension, splendidly efficacious. She seeks those who will serve her purpose, allowing full scope for human dedication, human heroism. So much is evident in the story of Christian Africa, which is a tale of unbeliev-able courage, sacrifice, immolation. But the nerve and fibre were Marian through and through.

In the same way we hope for a race of heroes in the great Russian adventure which is opening. The Heart of Mary will obtain for them wisdom and irre-sistible courage. The author here shows the signs along the way already traveled of Our Lady's delicate, sensitive watchfulness and her ready help. The links between the Papacy, Fatima and Russia are challeng-ing. It all began on May 13, 1917, the day of the first publicized apparition—there were others previously, we know. On that day Eugenio Pacelli was conse-crated bishop in Rome. As Pius XII he would be the first Pope of Fatima. On October 31, 1942, in the depth of world misery, he consecrated the Church and hu-mankind to the Immaculate Heart of Mary; on that oc-casion he included Russia as the land where Mary's icon was often hidden "awaiting better days." Ten years later, in the Encyclical *Sacro vergente anno* of July 7, 1952, addressed to all the Russian peoples, he made the consecration explicit, formally naming Russia. Paul VI renewed the general prayer of consecration, on November 21, 1964, at the end of the third session of Vatican II. Three years later, for the Fatima Golden Jubilee, he went to the sanctuary and met Lucia. He also issued for the occasion an important Marian text, *Signum Magnum*.

Meanwhile prayer mounted up from countless hearts, from many centers of piety and fervor, for the great intention. The Iron Curtain was less spoken of; but the Berlin Wall was still standing, a symbol of so much that was hidden, hurtful, oppressive far beyond its shadow. And then suddenly light appeared; the machinery of oppression seemed to crumble; Christ was abroad and welcomed in the land so recently closed to him. The lineal successor of Stalin made two visits to John Paul II, one Slav to another; he invited the Pope to Russia, offered diplomatic ties and promised a charter of religious freedom, now enacted. Then in the days of the "coup," all the world saw Mass on their television screens, offered for the young victims of repression.

Have the "better days" spoken of by Pius XII arrived? Can there now be no going back? Every reliable news item coming out of Russia prompts an optimistic answer to these questions. One of the most remarkable witnesses to religious life in the country in recent years must be heard, Tatiana Goricheva. A university lecturer, who lived the life of her milieu, she was converted to Christianity and joined the clandestine Christian feminist movement. Like all the members she was harried and victimized, reduced in status to that of a lift operator in a hotel. Finally she was given a choice between banishment—like Alexander Solzhenitsyn—or jail. Fortunately for us she chose exile. We have her records of the heroic minority within the fortress.

But we have happier tales. With the changed religious climate, Tatiana has gone back and found her beloved country athirst for God. Last year, at the annual session of the French Society for Marian Studies, she gave an eye-witness account of these wonders: of a Red Army colonel who told her of his conversion, one of many in his profession; of a television interviewer, who after two hours on religion still wanted her to go on; of people rejoicing that Russia's ancient title "House of Mary" has come alive again.

This testimony will be amplified in a book to appear shortly in the United States by a research worker, Michael Brown, already known for his splendid book on the exiled Ukrainian Catholic, Joseph Terelya; inmate of Soviet prisons for decades, witness to the apparitions of world-wide interest at Hrushiv in western Ukraine. These apparitions, sometimes drawing hundreds of thousands to the spot, began on the anniversary of the Chernobyl disaster! All over the Ukraine Michael found churches opened, being refurbished, everywhere the sense of a new era. Please God it will continue.

The distinguished Marian theologian, Fr. René Laurentin, specialist in apparitions and in the vast spectrum of contemporary Catholicism, has also assembled in a fascinating new book, *Les Chrétiens Détonateurs des Libérations a l'Est,* the results of his personal research through interviews conducted on the spot with some of the dominant, influential personalities in the religious revival in Russia and in the eastern countries just freed from Russian domination. Activists, prisoners of conscience, prelates—some also prisoners in their time—rulers, leaders, all pass before his sympathetic in-depth scrutiny.

To the desired change, which means so much for the world, John Paul II has, under God and with Our Lady's help, made a contribution of incalculable importance. His pastoral activity on behalf of the Russian people is rooted in a deeply spiritual outlook. This is seen especially in the magnificent dynamic theology of the Holy Spirit which he has taught. The great themes on the Spirit are expressed in his Encyclical *Dominum et Vivificantem,* the most important in the history of the Papacy, in the addresses on the occasion of the sixteenth centenary of the Council of Constantinople, which defined the divinity of the Holy Spirit, in the remarkable, lengthy passage in *Redemptoris Missio* on the Spirit as "principal agent of mission," in the extended series of catecheses on the great compelling doctrine, and many other moments enriched by inspiring insights equally relevant. John Paul II is the Pope of the Spirit, which adds a precious dimension to his Marian teaching, for "Mary and the Spirit" is one of the rewarding themes to challenge theologians since Vatican II. Within the body of thought thus evolving, the idea of the Heart of Mary has a wonderful place, making for an exciting synthesis. For John Paul II has enlarged the theology of the heart by the insights gained from his research in phenomenology .

In fact, the Pope gave vitality to a concept noted in Scripture and Tradition, renewed very recently at the instigation of a great prelate of the Far East, Cardinal Sin of Manila. His Eminence sponsored the International Symposium of the Two Hearts, taking for its title a phrase from John Paul II's discourses, "The Alliance of the Two Hearts." The meeting took place and the papers were presented by qualified experts over a comprehensive range of topics at Fatima in September 1986, and diffused to the public at Manila in the following year, all with ample, active support from the Pope: scholarship and cerebral activity of the highest kind there met the message more than once linked with Fatima. The first promise of the angel to the children spoke of the "merciful designs of the Hearts of Jesus and Mary." The ultimate glory to accrue to the Immaculate Heart, according to the Lord's revelation to Lucia, is that it will be honored along with his own Sacred Heart. What has been seen for generations on the Miraculous Medal is thus placed in a cosmic setting. Let us hope that the one-time victim of Nazism and Marxism, who has made the world his own, will live to see this triumph.

Michael O'Carroll, CSSp
November 18, 1991

1

THE ATTEMPT
ON THE LIFE
OF POPE JOHN PAUL II

WE LIVE IN TIMES OF DRAMATIC EVENTS, when the destinies of nations can be raised or reversed with unparalleled rapidity. The collapse of the Marxist tyranny of the former Soviet Union within less than a decade is one of the most extraordinary and unexpected reversals in modern history. Of the many explanations which have been put forward, few if any have given serious attention to the religious and spiritual issues posed by the sudden downfall of an avowedly atheistic and anti-Christian regime which, until the astonishing upheavals of the past decade, employed means of unprecedented violence and inhumanity, contrary to all accepted norms of behavior, in order to attain its ends.

My object in this study is to remedy that omission by examining the most significant of the signs, events

and testimonies of an unmistakably supernatural
character that have emerged in the decade from May
1981 to December 1991, in relation to the recent astonishing events in Central and Eastern Europe. I do not
seek to show that everything that has happened is
only explicable in terms of some sort of inevitable miracle or pre-determined religious fix, which disquali-
fies all the other social, economic and political factors
that have been at work. But I do maintain that it is impossible to achieve a proper understanding of the immense drama that is being played out if one omits or
fails to take proper account of the religious element in
the whole scenario. This is especially true of a country
like Russia, which until the year 1917 was steeped in
centuries of Christianity. It was then suddenly and
brutally overwhelmed by a revolutionary regime that
was bitterly and systematically hostile to religion; and
it was that malevolence towards the Church that led
in due course to the most audacious strike ever conceived against it: the attempt on the life of Pope John
Paul II in St. Peter's Square, Rome, on May 13, 1981.

And that is where this story begins. By the design
of Providence, that consummately evil act, epitomiz-
ing man's rejection and hatred of God, became instead
a dramatically visible sign of God's active presence in
the world through the medium of Mary, His Mother.
Her intervention, as John Paul II has acknowledged
several times, saved the life of the Pope. As I show in
the light of important new evidence which has only
recently been made public, we now know that the
failed assassination attempt set in motion a sequence

of events and signs of a supernatural character, which ran parallel to and closely interacted with the astonishing events that have unfolded in the past few years in Central and Eastern Europe. Once initiated, this process carried on, quietly working away on its own from within, to culminate in the return of President Gorbachev on August 22, 1991 and the ensuing collapse of Communism. It is precisely the date of August 22 which is so remarkable, for it cannot have been outside the design of Providence that the coup to restore the former atheistic regime collapsed on the day when the Church's liturgy honors Mary as the Queen of Heaven and earth. As we shall see, the political denouement that transpired in that decisive week was accompanied by a number of supernatural signs. This indeed was perhaps to be expected, for Jesus told the disciples, when He appeared to them after the Resurrection, that "signs will be associated with those who believe" (Mk 16:17).

The evidence examined in this study points conclusively to a link between these recent events and the revelations about the destiny of Russia made in 1917 to three shepherd children by a "Lady from Heaven," in a remote mountain village in Portugal. It is clear that Mary's promise that Russia would return to God is by no means yet fulfilled, but it is equally indisputable that the former regime's fanatical persecution of the Church has been brought to an end. When the two most powerful men in the Soviet Union were interviewed live on American television, in the aftermath of the coup, as they sat in gilded armchairs in the Kremlin's St. George's Hall, President Yeltsin admitted: "This experiment was a tragedy for our people and it was too bad that it happened on our territory," and President Gorbachev openly confessed that "the historical experience we have accumulated has allowed us to . . . say in a decisive fashion that the model has failed" (*Daily Telegraph*, September 7, 1991; *New York Times*, same date). President Yeltsin has also stated, in an interview in *Izvestia*, an extract of which was printed in *The Irish Catholic* of October 24, 1991: "I have the greatest respect for the Orthodox Church, for its history, its contribution to Russian spiritual life, its moral teachings, its tradition of mercy and charity. Today, the Church is moving ahead in these areas and our duty is, in turn, to re-establish the rights of the Church. . . ."

It is the opinion of many eminent Catholic authorities, including the Holy Father, that in these unprecedented happenings we may now discern the beginnings of the long-awaited intervention which Mary foretold at Fatima in 1917. These events have clear implications for the Church, as it stands on the verge of the third millennium in circumstances which have changed dramatically since 1981. I therefore conclude this study with a brief survey of John Paul II's most recent addresses at Fatima, in which he sets out his vision for the future.

As I have said, Pope John Paul II himself was made the subject of an extraordinary sign, when he was permitted to suffer the assassination attempt in 1981 on precisely the same day—May 13—that Mary first appeared at Fatima in 1917. Recognizing the significance of this date himself, the Holy Father has been to Fatima twice to thank Our Lady for saving his life. Most recently, on May 13, 1991, in his moving Act of Entrustment, he acclaimed the Blessed Virgin as "My mother forever, and especially on May 13, 1981 when I felt your helpful presence at my side." Is not Our Lady's intervention to save his life, and the Pope's open recognition of her helpful presence at his side, a visible sign that we the faithful should turn to Mary too, in these times of confusion and trial, to implore the intercession of the Mother of God whenever we find ourselves in difficulty and danger?

Another sign imprinted in the evil act which sought to take the life of John Paul II in 1981, is the association of the Holy Father, in his own person, with the suffering and sin of the world. In the homily he delivered on his first visit to Fatima, on May 13, 1982, exactly one year after the assassination attempt, the Holy Father openly confessed. "My heart is oppressed when I see the sin of the world and the whole range of menaces gathering like a dark cloud over mankind." However, he continued vigorously, the love of God is more powerful than any evil, hence "no 'sin of the world' can ever overcome this love." Those words have a particularly poignant ring, for while they are addressed to the Church and the whole world, they are also applicable to his own person. The whole world caught its breath when the Vicar of Christ himself was struck by the "sin of the world," causing him to shed his blood and suffer. By this act, God permitted John Paul II to partake in his own person in the suffering of all those who fall victim to sin and evil. It

was on that same day, in 1917, one recalls, that Our
Lady first appeared to the children, and asked them:
"Are you willing to offer yourselves to God and bear
all the sufferings He wills to send you, as an act of
reparation for the sins by which He is offended? . . ."
"Yes, we are willing," they replied. "Then you are
going to have much to suffer. . . ." Finally, by the remarkable circumstances of his own deliverance from
the assassin's bullet, are not the Pope's words also a
living vindication of his deep personal faith in the su-
premacy of God's love, which no "sin of the world"
can ever overcome, a love which is obtained through
consecration to the heart of the Mother?

Events have developed with dramatic rapidity
over the past decade, and one is inclined to forget that
President Ronald Reagan of the United States and
Prime Minister Margaret Thatcher of Great Britain
both suffered similar horrific assassination attempts,
in March 1981 and October 1984 respectively. Ten
years ago, the political, military and ideological ten-
sions between the powers were far more grim and ac-
centuated than is the case today. Europe was still in
the icy grip of the cold war; Soviet tanks menaced the
Polish border; the Church was prostrate under ruth-
less atheistic persecution; Lech Walesa, the Solidarity
leader who is now President of Poland, was in prison
in solitary confinement near the Russian border; people were shot for trying to escape from the East over
the Berlin wall; Mrs. Thatcher had only recently come
to power in Great Britain; President Gorbachev and

his policies of glasnost and perestroika were all un-heard of; and no one could then have foreseen the in-credible collapse—auto-dissolution, indeed—of the whole Communist ethos and power structure that would occur at the end of the decade.

The fall of the old hardline regime was not to pass entirely without a shot being fired, but it is interesting to note that the two most determined strikes mounted by militant atheism in an attempt to preserve the sta-tus quo, the coup against President Gorbachev and the attempt on the life of the Pope, actually brought to pass the complete opposite of their intended ends. It was the failure of the Marxist coup on August 19, 1991, seeking to extinguish the fledgling liberalization of Communism, which thereby inexorably propelled Mikhail Gorbachev to preside over the liquidation of the Communist Party and the former Soviet Union. And it was the failure of the atheist-inspired bullet to procure the assassination of Pope John Paul II in St. Peter's Square on May 13, 1981 that led the Holy Fa-ther to fulfill the request for the consecration of Russia to Mary's Immaculate Heart in March 1984, as the first step towards the deliverance of Russia from atheism and its eventual return to God.

The event which immediately followed the assas-sination attempt was the period the Pope spent in the hospital. In the light of information from an authori-tative source close to John Paul II, which has only re-cently been made public, it can now be seen that, as regards the development of the Fatima message in the

Church, this period was the decisive turning-point in John Paul's pontificate. Owing to the gravity of his wounds, the Pope was compelled to spend a considerable period in the hospital. We now know, from an interview published in the authoritative journal, *30 Days*, that Our Lady of Fatima's intervention on May 13, 1981 accomplished more than just saving the Pope's life. In an article entitled "MIRACLE IN THE EAST—Is the collapse of Communism due to the intervention of the Virgin Mary? Is the prophecy of Fatima being fulfilled?" which was published in the March 1990 issue of the magazine, the reader is given a remarkably frank and revealing insight into some of John Paul II's personal views and initiatives on Fatima during the period he spent in the hospital in 1981.

Pavol Hnilica is a Slovak bishop who was secretly consecrated and then spent years in Communist concentration camps. While John Paul II was convalescing in the hospital, he asked Bishop Hnilica to send him all the documents related to Fatima and the Marian apparitions. "I brought them to him," said Hnilica. "Some of the texts were originals. *He read everything with extreme attention* (my emphasis). Even as a cardinal, Wojtyla had carried a petition to the Vatican, in the name of the Polish bishops, to ask again for the consecration of Russia. When John Paul II left the hospital, I brought a statue of Our Lady of Fatima to him at Castel Gandolfo. *He had a small church constructed in Poland, in a forest on the border with the Soviet Union, to house that statue. It is there now, in the exact position John Paul II wanted it in: with its gaze directed toward Russia*" (my emphasis; from *30 Days*, March 1990, page 13).

This statement by Bishop Hnilica is very informative, and helps us to recreate a scenario which although only speculative, can nevertheless be seen to be close to reality. The Pope is shot, on the precise anniversary date of Our Lady's first apparition at Fatima in 1917. Despite the enormity of the act, it was planned and executed with such cold and calculating precision, that the would-be murderer asked the Pope, when John Paul II went to see him in prison later: "Why didn't you die? I know that my aim was true, and I know that the bullet was very powerful and mortal . . . so why didn't you die?" John Paul replied: "One hand fired the shot, another guided it" (quoted in *Fatima-Moscou*, Editions Tequi, Paris, November 1991, page 54). Ten years later, in his Act of Entrustment at Fatima, John Paul II acclaimed Mary as "my mother for ever, and *especially on May 13, 1981, when I felt your helpful presence at my side*" (my emphasis). So he knew, therefore, at that dire moment, that it was Our Lady who intervened to save his life. But he was not spared the physical consequences of the bullet which entered his body, and owing to the gravity of his wounds, he was obliged to spend a lengthy period in the hospital. It was during those months, we now know from Bishop Hnilica, when providentially the Pope had time at his disposal, that he asked for *all* the documents related to Fatima, some of which were *original texts,* and *read everything with extreme attention* (my emphasis).

We are not told precisely what it was that the Pope wanted to know, or what caused him to examine all that documentation so meticulously, but it seems evident that there must have been a specific reason which led him to do so; and this development, coming so soon after the attempt on his life, while he was still recuperating in the hospital, was clearly a consequence of the dramatic sign he had received from Our Lady on May 13. Hnilica's reference to the petition for the consecration of Russia, which John Paul had brought to the Vatican as Cardinal Wojtyla, shows that he already knew of the grave significance of that act.

But now that he himself was Pope, and had just been made the subject of a clear sign from Our Lady of Fatima, he was in a position to send for *all* the documents concerning the apparitions, including some original texts, which perhaps he did not know about or had not been able to consult previously. There was, for example, the lengthy work of Fr. Joaquin Alonso, CMF, which had been commissioned by the Bishop of Fatima in 1966. After many meetings with Portuguese and Spanish scholars, including Fr. Alonso himself, Bishop Alberto Amaral of Leiria-Fatima concluded that Fr. Alonso's work should not be published by the Sanctuary because it was not a critical edition.

But the work begun by Fr. Alonso has been carried on, and Fr. Antonio N. Martins, SJ, one of the leading authorities on Fatima in Portugal, has recently informed me that a commission of Portuguese scholars is preparing the critical edition of Fatima documents, the first volume of which is to appear soon.

Bishop Hnilica's revelation, in this article in *30 Days*, clearly indicates the importance which Fatima had come to assume in the thinking of the Pope, following the attempt on his life. Then, in a further paragraph on page 14 of the same article, Hnilica quotes the Pope's own views on Fatima, as expressed to him by John Paul when he was leaving the hospital. What the Holy Father says is extremely illuminating, and I reproduce the whole paragraph in which his personal views are quoted:

> Does the Pope, too, therefore, believe that the events currently unfolding in the East bloc in some way relate to the promises of Fatima? (asks the author of the article, writing in March 1990). There are some who think so, like Bishop Hnilica: "Yes, the Pope is convinced of it. When he left the hospital, he said to me: *'I have come to understand that the only way to save the world from war, to save it from atheism, is the conversion of Russia according to the message of Fatima'* (my emphasis). "This is in some way coming to pass," continued Bishop Hnilica, "but it demands that we bear our part of the responsibility. The process is not automatic."

This conclusion of the Holy Father is strong, decisive, and final. It does not admit of any alternative solution. By his use of the phrase "come to understand," it is clear that the Holy Father must have reached this conclusion, which he then proceeded to annunciate, as a result of the intense study of the subject which he had undertaken in the hospital. If one puts this conclusion alongside the revelation to the children on July 13, 1917, in which Our Lady foretold the future course of the world, for good or for evil, it would appear that John Paul II is reiterating in his own words the key operative part of Mary's request at Fatima for the consecration of Russia to her Immaculate Heart by the Pope:

... If what I say to you is done, many souls will be saved and there will be peace. The war is going to end (this refers to the First World War); but if people do not cease offending God, a worse one will break out during the pontificate of Pius XI (this refers to the Second World War). When you see a night illuminated by an unknown light, know that this is the sign given you by God that he is about to punish the world for its crimes, by means of war, famine, and persecutions of the Church and of the Holy Father.

To prevent this, I shall come to ask for the consecration of Russia to my Immaculate Heart, and the Communion of Reparation on the First Saturdays. If my requests are heeded, Russia will be converted and there will be peace; if not, she will spread her errors throughout the world, causing wars and persecutions of the Church. The good will be martyred, the Holy Father will have much to suffer, various nations will be annihilated. In the end, my Immaculate Heart will triumph. The Holy Father will consecrate Russia to me, and she will be converted, and a period of peace will he granted to the world ... (from *Fatima in Lucia's Own Words*, page 162).

In the first and last sentences of the second paragraph above, which is taken from the great prophecy of July 1917, Our Lady requests the collegial consecration of Russia. In 1981 this had still not yet been carried out in the way required by God; although, as John Paul II would have noted when he was studying all the Fatima documents, consecrations to the Immaculate Heart of Mary had already been made by his predecessors Pius XII, in 1942 and 1952, and Paul VI, in 1964 and 1967. It was the urgent necessity of carrying out this act, because he had come to understand that it was "the only way to save the world from war, to save it from atheism," that John Paul expressed to Bishop Hnilica on leaving the hospital. Hence it came about that on May 13, 1982, the first anniversary of the attempt on his life, Pope John Paul II carried out a solemn and public Act of Consecration of the whole world, including Russia, to the Immaculate Heart of Mary, with the intention, clearly expressed in the opening paragraphs of the Act, of effecting it in collegial union with all the bishops of the Church.

The conclusion seems manifest, therefore, that it was the attempt on the life of John Paul, inspired by a militantly atheistic regime that sensed in his pontificate the rise of a force determined to resist its own global schemes and ambitions, which providentially brought the Pope to a deeper understanding of the grave significance of the consecration of Russia, requested by Our Lady at Fatima, and the consequent determination to bring about Russia's conversion through its consecration to Mary's Immaculate Heart.

Before going on to review the Act of Consecration of May 13, 1982 in the next chapter, there is one further revealing insight on which to comment, in the first interview with Bishop Hnilica in the article cited from *30 Days* above. I refer to the touching story of how John Paul II ordered the construction of a small church in Poland, in a forest on the Soviet border, to house the

Pope John Paul II before the statue of Our Lady of Fatima

statue which Hnilica had taken to the Pope. He gave exact directions as to how he wanted it positioned in the chapel, "with its gaze directed towards Russia." There is a wholly spiritual quality in this inspired act, by its simplicity, its expression of trusting devotion, its concealment from the eyes of all save Heaven. It recalls similar gestures of confidence in the intercessory power of the Virgin Mother which were often seen throughout Europe in the ages of faith.

Devotion to Mary in medieval England, for example, was such that throughout all Europe, England was commonly known as "Our Lady's dowry," as the Archbishop of Canterbury stated in a mandate issued from Lambeth Palace in 1399. One has only to speak of Catholic Poland to think immediately of the great shrine of Our Lady of Czestochowa, where at Jasna Gora, the "bright mountain," there is venerated the celebrated image of the Black Madonna, long claimed by popular tradition to have been painted by St. Luke. And is perhaps one reason why Portugal was so specially favored by the Queen of Heaven at Fatima in this century that in 1646 King John IV of Portugal laid down his crown at the feet of Our Lady of the Immaculate Conception and proclaimed her Patroness of his kingdom?

It is not possible to measure the significance of this gesture of John Paul II, but we may surely surmise that it was one of those imaginative and bold acts of devotion to which only a heart filled with the true love of the Mother of God can rise. Heart to heart, *Totus tuus!* As such, and coming from the person of the

Vicar of Christ, it speaks more powerfully than any
words about John Paul II's desire and intention to fulfill the request of Our Lady of Fatima with regard to
the conversion of Russia.

There is a celebrated photograph of the Holy Father at Castel Gandolfo, with his hand over his heart,
slightly bent forward and looking as if he was "in conversation" with the serenely beautiful and appealing
statue of Our Lady which is standing just in front of
him. That image was the one brought to him by
Bishop Hnilica when John Paul II left the hospital, and
it was a replica of the statue of the Immaculate Heart
of Mary that was sculpted under Sister Lucia's direction, and which may be seen in her convent in Coimbra. I know this photograph well, and I have also seen
the image in the convent where Sister Lucia still lives,
but it was not until I came to reflect further on the
meaning of the Holy Father's gesture that I noticed
there is one significant difference between these two
statues.

The head of the statue in Sister Lucia's convent is
unadorned. But, as may be clearly seen from the photograph, the statue brought by Bishop Hnilica to John
Paul and placed by the Pope in the church on the Soviet-Polish border bears a rich crown. To anticipate
briefly the events that I describe much more fully in
chapter four, it is remarkable that the coup to remove
President Gorbachev and re-instate hardline Communism finally collapsed—and with it, in rapid succes-
sion thereafter, the whole Communist ethos and
system—on *August 22*, the date on which the Church

now celebrates the Feast of the Queenship of Mary. (August 22 was formerly the Feast of the Immaculate Heart of Mary.) It is remarkable, because the statue which John Paul II had placed on the Soviet-Polish border ten years before in 1981, "with its gaze directed toward Russia," was not the Pilgrim Virgin of the *Capelinha*, or Chapel of the Apparitions at Fatima, but the image of Our Lady displaying her Immaculate Heart and bearing the crown, symbol of her Queenship—precisely those two titles under which Mary has been invoked by the Church on her Feast day of August 22!

In 1981, however, the Church was still prostrate under atheistic persecution, the Holy Father himself had been the subject of a horrific assassination attempt and the cold war was a grim reality of superpower politics. There were as yet no visible signs of the astonishing changes that were to shake the whole continent of Europe barely a decade later. The consecration to the Immaculate Heart of Mary by John Paul II in 1984 was destined to set those changes in motion, and that is the subject of the next chapter.

2

THE CONSECRATION OF RUSSIA BY POPE JOHN PAUL II

The Act of Consecration of May 13, 1982

As we have seen, the Pope decided to go to Fatima on the anniversary of the assassination attempt, to thank Our Lady for saving his life, and to carry out the Collegial Consecration.

Was it John Paul II's inner conviction—that the conversion of Russia according to the message of Fatima was the only way to save the world from war and from atheism—which accounts for the personal, almost heart-to-heart expression of his appeal to the "Mother of individuals and peoples" in the Act of Consecration, and the longing with which he came to carry it out? That we do not know; but one cannot fail to be touched by the sense of urgency in the Pope's words:

18

... O Mother of individuals and peoples ... you who have a mother's awareness of all the struggles between good and evil, between light and darkness, which afflict the modern world, accept the cry which we, as though moved by the Holy Spirit, address directly to your Heart ... Before you, Mother of Christ, before your Immaculate Heart, I today, together with the whole Church, unite myself with our Redeemer in this his consecration for the world and for people, which only in his divine Heart has the power to obtain pardon and to secure reparation. The power of this consecration lasts for all time and embraces all individuals, peoples and nations. It overcomes every evil that the spirit of darkness is able to awaken, and has in fact awakened in our times, in the heart of man and in his history ... Oh, how deeply we feel the need for consecration on the part of humanity and of the world—our modern world—in union with Christ himself!

O Immaculate Heart! Help us to conquer the menace of evil which so easily takes root in the hearts of the people of today, and whose immeasurable effects already weigh down upon our modern world and seem to block the path towards the future! From famine and war, deliver us. From nuclear war, from incalculable self-destruction, from every kind of war, deliver us. ... Accept, O Mother of Christ, this cry laden with the sufferings of all individual human beings, laden with the sufferings of whole societies. Let there be revealed once more in the history of the world the infinite power of merciful Love. May it put a stop to evil. May it transform consciences. May your Immaculate Heart reveal for all the light of Hope!

The homily which John Paul II delivered on this occasion was the Pope's first major pronouncement on Fatima since the attempt on his life, and in it he sets out a lucid explanation of the role of the Mother of Christ in society, and thence, of the significance of consecrating the world to her Immaculate Heart:

> The Immaculate Heart of Mary, opened with the words, "Woman, behold your Son," is spiritually united with the heart of her Son, opened by the soldier's spear. . . . Consecrating the world to the Immaculate Heart of Mary means returning beneath the Cross of the Son. It means consecrating the world to the pierced heart of the Savior, bringing it back to the very source of its Redemption. . . .
>
> The appeal of the Lady of the Message of Fatima is so deeply rooted in the Gospel and the whole of Tradition that the Church feels that the message imposes a commitment on her. . . . Today John Paul II . . . reads it again with trepidation in his heart because he sees how many people and societies—how many Christians—have gone in the opposite direction to the one indicated in the message of Fatima. Sin has thus made itself firmly at home in the world, and denial of God has become widespread in the ideologies, ideas and plans of human beings. . . .

But for this very reason the evangelical call to repentance and conversion, uttered in the Mother's message, remains . . . still more relevant . . . still more urgent. . . . My heart is oppressed when I see the sin of the world and the whole range of menaces gathering like a dark cloud over mankind, but it also rejoices with hope as I once more do what has been done by my predecessors, when they consecrated the world to the heart of the Mother. . . . Doing this means consecrating the world to Him who is infinite holiness. This holiness means redemption, it means a love more powerful than evil. No "sin of the world" can ever overcome this love. . . . The heart of the mother is aware of this, more than any other heart in the universe, visible, and invisible. And so she calls us. . . .

In the person of John Paul II, God has brought to the chair of Peter a Pope of remarkable gifts and abilities. One of his endearing characteristics is the simple way in which he does not refrain to lay bare before the Church the thoughts that are exercising his heart about matters of moment affecting the salvation of mankind, and this engaging openness is manifest in a remarkable way in the above passages. One has only to read these words to realize that the Pope sees, the Pope knows, the Pope *understands* the true state of the world today because his vision is expressed humbly and simply *from the heart,* a heart which is profoundly centered in the love of God; and also because it is touchingly evident that as Vicar of Christ, charged with a grave responsibility for the salvation of mankind—a mission of which he is deeply conscious—his words are addressed *to the heart,* to the heart of the Mother made manifest at Fatima.

In the first place, then, the message of Fatima is "so deeply rooted in the Gospel," the Holy Father tells us, that it *"imposes a commitment on her"* (my emphasis), and his words that follow about the grave presence of sin and the denial of God in the world show clearly why this is so. And secondly, from the above passages it can be seen that, at the center of its mystery, Fatima is an affair of the heart. One might even say that it is a contest between hearts: the heart of Mary, Mother of God, on the one hand, intervening on behalf of all mankind at Fatima, to reveal a new outpouring of God's love for his noblest creation; and the hearts of modern men on the other hand, so many of whom spurn their Creator's loving attention, and in consequence spread all around them in society, despite so much material brilliance, the lamentable disorders of sin.

It is important to read the entire text of this moving homily, which is printed in full as Appendix III, for a correct understanding of the development of Fatima in the succeeding years of John Paul II's pontificate. For the moment it is sufficient to note that in it one finds the same predominant theme to which the Pope returns in his addresses at Fatima in May 1991: the troubling presence of sin and evil in the world, against which there stands the power of the consecration to the heart of the Mother, which means a love more powerful than any evil, and which no sin of this world can ever overcome.

God must certainly have been pleased with this consecration, for this was the first time in the history of the Fatima revelations that it had been carried out solemnly and publicly by the Holy Father with the intention, clearly expressed in the opening paragraphs of the Act, of effecting it in collegial union with all the bishops of the Church. However, the letters which had been sent to the world's bishops, inviting them to join with John Paul II in the consecration, arrived too late for them to be able to participate in the ceremony, and in consequence this act did not perfectly fulfill the request of Our Lady, as Sister Lucia told the Apostolic Nuncio in Portugal after the consecration.

The Act of Consecration of March 25, 1984

John Paul II accepted that it was necessary to repeat the consecration in order to ensure that it would be truly collegial. Accordingly, on December 8, 1983, the Feast of the Immaculate Conception, the Pope sent a letter to all the bishops of the world, Catholic and Orthodox, asking them to join him in making the Act of Consecration to the Immaculate Heart of Mary on March 25, 1984, the Feast of the Annunciation. The Holy Father enclosed the prayer to be used, and this included in itself the two important acts of consecration which had been made by his predecessor, Pius XII, who was known as the "Pope of Fatima" because he had been consecrated bishop at the precise moment Our Lady was appearing to the children in Portugal, on May 13, 1917.

In response to the appeal of Our Lady, Pope Pius XII had made the first consecration of the whole world to her Immaculate Heart on October 31, 1942 (printed in full in Appendix I), in the course of which, referring to Russia, he stated: "To those peoples separated from us by error or schism, above all, to those who show a special devotion to you, and where there was no home that did not honor your venerable icon—though now it may be hidden and put away for better days—give peace and lead them back to the one fold of Christ under the one true Shepherd." Ten years later, on July 7, 1952, the feast of Saints Cyril and Methodius, the apostles of the Slavs, Pius XII made a specific consecration of the peoples of Russia, in his apostolic letter *Sacro Vergente Anno* (see extracts printed in Appendix II): ". . . Just as some years ago we consecrated the whole human race to the Immaculate Heart of the Virgin Mary, Mother of God, so today we consecrate and we dedicate in a very special manner all the peoples of Russia to this Immaculate Heart. . . ."

Both these acts were very important, because they signified the acceptance by the Sovereign Pontiff of Our Lady of Fatima's request for the consecration of Russia. However, because they were consecrations effected purely by the Pope in his individual capacity, they only partially fulfilled this request. The consecration of John Paul II in 1984 remedied this deficiency. Paragraphs three and four of the act clearly stated that it was to be carried out in collegial union with all the bishops of the Church: "We find ourselves united with all the Pastors of the Church in a particular bond whereby we constitute a body and a college, just as by Christ's wish the Apostles constituted a body and college with Peter. In the bond of this union, we utter the words of the present Act, in which we wish to include, once more, the Church's hopes and anxieties for the modern world." Ample time of more than three months was allowed for the Pope's letter to reach all parts of the world, and so every bishop was notified in advance of the forthcoming consecration, and invited to join with the Pope in making it.

The statue of Our Lady was brought to Rome from the Chapel of the Apparitions at Fatima, and the Collegial Consecration, which substantially repeats the text of the Act of Consecration at Fatima of May 1982, was duly effected in front of St. Peter's Basilica on the Feast of the Annunciation, March 25, 1984. (The Act is printed in full in Appendix IV.) After this consecration, Sister Lucia was visited by the Apostolic Nuncio, who asked her: "'Is Russia now consecrated?' 'Yes, now it is,' I answered. The Nuncio then said: 'Now we wait for the miracle.' I answered, 'God will keep his word.'" (from an interview with Sister Lucia published in *Fatima Family Messenger*, October–December 1989, page 7). Bishop Alberto Cosme do Amaral of Leiria-Fatima told Fr. Robert Fox, the editor of *Fatima Family Messenger*, on July 10, 1989: "During the actual consecration by Pope John Paul II there were a few moments of pausing during which it was not clear

Pope John Paul II peforms the Consecration in Rome, March 25, 1984

what the Holy Father said. I thanked the Pope later for consecrating the world to the Immaculate Heart of Mary and the Pope added, 'and Russia.'" Bishop Amaral then said to Fr. Fox, "A moral totality of the world's bishops joined the Pope in this collegial consecration, including Eastern Orthodox bishops."

The Holy See, the Bishop of Leiria-Fatima, and leading Portuguese experts have all recently affirmed that the 1984 consecration satisfied the request of the Mother of God. Sister Lucia herself has issued several public statements in writing in the past two years, strongly affirming that the consecration was made in 1984 and that God has accepted it. The prominent international Catholic journal, *30 Days*, informed its readers, on page 13 of the issue of March 1990, that Sister Lucia "agreed to give *30 Days* three letters she wrote in recent months on the debated topic of the consecration of Russia to the Immaculate Heart of Mary. In all three, Sister Lucia recognizes as 'valid' the consecration carried out by John Paul II on March 25, 1984."

On the same page, *30 Days* published the complete text of one of these letters, written at Coimbra on November 21, 1989, in which Sister Lucia first explained that previous consecrations had not been effective because they had not been carried out "in union with all the bishops." Sister Lucia then said:

It was later made by the present pontiff, John Paul II, on 25 March 1984, after he wrote to all the bishops of the world, asking that each of them make the consecration in his own diocese with the people of God who had been entrusted to him. The Pope asked that the statue of Our Lady of Fatima be brought to Rome, and he did it publicly in union with all the bishops who with His Holiness were uniting themselves with the people of God, the Mystical Body of Christ; and it was made to the Immaculate Heart of Mary, Mother of Christ and of His Mystical Body, so that, with her and through her with Christ, the consecration could be carried and offered to the Father for the salvation of humanity.

Thus the consecration was made by His Holiness John Paul II on 25 March 1984.

Sister Lucia's whole life and testimony is above reproach. She has been publicly received by two popes, and her status as a seer must surely be as eminent as that of any other in this century, if not higher. Is it possible that she could be mistaken about an act of exceptional significance for the Church, and which she had been specially chosen by Heaven to request of the Holy Father? How many saints in the history of the Church have been granted a vision of the Mystery of the Holy Trinity as she was, on June 13, 1929? "It was at this time," as she wrote in her moving account of this exceptional grace, on pages 199–200 of her memoirs, *Fatima in Lucia's Own Words,* "that Our Lady informed me that the moment had come in which she wished me to make known to Holy Church her desire for the Consecration of Russia, and her promise to convert it. The communication was as follows:

13-6-1929. I had sought and obtained permission from my superiors and confessor to make a Holy Hour from eleven o'clock until midnight, every Thursday to Friday night. Being alone one night, I knelt near the altar rails in the middle of the chapel and, prostrate, I prayed the prayers of the Angel. Feeling tired, I then stood up and continued to say the prayers with my arms in the form of a cross. The only light was that of the sanctuary lamp. Suddenly the whole chapel was illuminated by a supernatural light, and above the altar appeared a cross of light, reaching to the ceiling. In a brighter light, on the upper part of the cross, could be seen the face of a man and his body as far as the waist; upon his breast was a dove of light; nailed to the cross was the body of another man. A little below the waist, I could see a chalice and a large host suspended in the air, on to which drops of blood were falling from the face of Jesus Crucified and from the wound in His side. These drops ran down on to the cross and fell into the chalice. Beneath the right arm of the cross was Our Lady and in her hand was her Immaculate Heart. (It was Our Lady of Fatima, with her Immaculate Heart in her left hand, without sword or roses, but with a crown of thorns and flames). Under the left arm of the cross, large letters, as if of crystal clear water which ran down upon the altar, formed these words: "Grace and Mercy."

I understood that it was the Mystery of the most Holy Trinity which was shown to me, and I received lights about this mystery which I am not permitted to reveal. Our Lady then said to me: "The moment has come in which God asks the Holy Father, in union with all the Bishops of the world, to make the consecration of Russia to my Immaculate Heart, promising to save it by this means." . . . I gave an account of this to the confessor, who ordered me to write down what Our Lady wanted done. Later, in an intimate communication, Our Lord complained to me, saying: "They did not wish to heed my request. Like the King of France, they will repent and do it, but it will be late. Russia will already have spread her errors throughout the world, provoking wars, and persecutions of the Church; the Holy Father will have much to suffer."

The 1984 consecration was "in union with all the bishops"

A considerable body of evidence, showing that this Consecration did indeed fulfill the request of Our Lady, is contained in seven articles by leading authorities on the subject, as originally published in the journals *Fatima Family Messenger* and *30 Days*, and which are available as a pamphlet from Augustine Publishing Company, issued in May 1990, and entitled *The Collegial Consecration of Russia is Accomplished*. In one of these articles, entitled "The Problem of the Consecration," Fr. Messias Coelho answers the questions raised by those who still doubt whether the 1984 consecration was carried out in the way required by God. Fr. Coelho is professor in a seminary in Portugal, and

a noted scholar, lecturer and expert on Fatima, and the
following passages contain the key points of his argu-
ment:

> Pope John Paul II informed all the bishops (by
> letter in ample time) what he was going to do and
> asked all bishops to join him in the Consecration.
> The Consecration of 25 March 1984 was therefore a
> world-wide, solemn, public collective act . . .
>
> As for the rest, it is worthwhile to take into ac-
> count the words of the Blessed Virgin which belong
> within the scope of the secret. We should consider
> the consecration as authentic and accomplished
> when looked at within the context of the literal in-
> terpretation of the words then spoken. Our Lady
> declared: "God asks the Holy Father, *in union with*
> all the bishops of the world, to make the consecra-
> tion . . ." Our Lady did not say: "God asks all the
> bishops of the world to make the consecration *with*
> the Holy Father" (emphasized as in the original).
> That would be very different. In the words of the
> Mother of God, there is an exigency for union. What
> kind of union? Physical union of persons? Of place?
> Of time? By no means. Union, equivalent to repeti-
> tion, amplification, imitation? It is also not easy to
> find any evidence for that.
>
> What is certainly included in this expression
> (of Our Lady) "in union with all the bishops" is its
> essential element, or rather, a union of the spirit,
> union of the intelligence and heart, in charity and

intention, so as to honor the Blessed Mother and to acknowledge her active presence in the world of which the public recitation of the formula of Consecration is a worthy outward manifestation. This element was present, but only in a partial way in the Consecrations of Pius XII and Paul VI, which were not previously announced before being made. The intention was well expressed in that of Pope John Paul II. It was thus that the act of Pope John Paul II (1984) had the decisive importance to fulfill the conditions requested.

As for the object of the Consecration—Russia— a fundamental axiom of philosophy is forgotten by those who require a new consecration: "the more contains the less," or "the whole contains the sum of its parts." Russia is part of the world. Russia is included in the Consecration although the text (used by the Pope) does not mention Russia explicitly. From the words of the Blessed Virgin, one could by no means conclude that she demanded an act exclusively centered on that country alone.

The message of Fatima, however is not exhausted in the request for the Consecration of Russia. The Fatima message is much more vast and implies above all the personal involvement of each one of us in the totality of its message. It is the living of the Fatima message . . . that should guide all movements claiming to have their origin in the Fatima message . . .

Theologically the problem is clearer. The apparitions and their messages are charisms, i.e., acts of the Holy Spirit. Their interpretation—to be correct—has to be also an act of the Holy Spirit. He is the Soul of the Church. So, the only correct interpretation is that of the Church and not that of seers. Usually the charism of seers consists only in receiving and telling the Church what they saw and heard . . ." (from *The Collegial Consecration of Russia is Accomplished*, pages 4–6, where the article of Fr. Messias Coelho is printed in full).

By his intention in repeating the act in 1984, to ensure that this time it would be carried out in a way that was truly collegial; by his words inviting the bishops to join with him in making it; and by his action, in notifying every bishop in the world of the forthcoming consecration and giving them ample time to join with him, John Paul II for his part indubitably fulfilled the request of Our Lady for the Holy Father to make the consecration "in union with all the bishops. " Thus, as Sister Lucia says, *"the Pope was united to all the bishops in 1984"* (my emphasis), and it is that union— the union of the head of the Mystical Body on earth with all its members—which is the one that was specified in the request of Our Lady, as Sister Lucia also observed (*ibid.*, page 8). This is evident from the words of Our Lady, which defined the order in which the act itself was to be carried out, namely: by "the Holy Father, in union with all the bishops of the world," and not vice versa, by the bishops of all the world, in union with the Holy Father, as Fr. Messias Coelho has pointed out (*ibid.*, page 4).

In a letter dated May 18, 1936, Sister Lucia re-counts an intimate communication with Our Lord in which He explains this requirement, that the act of consecration should he carried out "in union with all the bishops:"

> ... Intimately, I have spoken to Our Lord about the subject (the consecration of Russia), and not too long ago I asked Him why He would not convert Russia without the Holy Father making that conse-cration. (He replied) "Because I want *My whole Church* (my emphasis) to acknowledge that conse-cration as a triumph of the Immaculate Heart of Mary, so that it may extend its cult later on and put the devotion to the Immaculate Heart beside the de-votion to My Sacred Heart ... Pray much for the Holy Father. He will do it, but it will be late. Never-theless, the Immaculate Heart of Mary will save Russia. It has been entrusted to her." (*Memoirs and Letters of Sister Lucia,* edited by Fr. Antonio Martins, SJ, 1973, page 415).

It is true that a number of bishops did not unite in making the consecration with the Holy Father in 1984, and it cannot be doubted that the act would have been more pleasing to God if they had been so united. Clearly there is an implicit desire for such union by all the bishops with the Holy Father, and in view of the wonderful graces which God wishes to give the world through the Immaculate Heart of Mary, one cannot understand why any bishop should not wish to comply with Our Lady's request. The preservation of Portugal from involvement in the Second World War is one of the clearest demonstrations of the power of this consecration. The bishops of Portugal solemnly consecrated their country to the Immaculate Heart of Mary on May 13, 1938, and they renewed this act on December 8, 1940, at the request of Sister Lucia, in the cathedral of Lisbon. Sister Lucia mentioned it in a letter to Pius XII dated December 2, 1940: "Most Holy Father . . . Our Lord promises to give a special protection to our country during this war, in consideration of the consecration which the Reverend Bishops of Portugal have made of the nation to the Immaculate Heart of Mary. And this protection will be the proof of the graces which God would give to the other nations if, like Portugal, they were to consecrate themselves to it." It is a matter of history that Portugal was preserved from involvement in World War II, in fulfillment of Our Lord's promise.

Nevertheless, this absence of union on the part of some bishops does not by itself invalidate the act, because, as I have demonstrated above, the literal reading and interpretation of Our Lady's words clearly establishes that her formal request was directed specifically to "the Holy Father, in union with all the bishops," in that order, and not the reverse, as Fr. Messias Coelho observed. Hence it cannot be argued, from the words of Our Lady, that the act was not accepted by God, purely on account of those bishops who did not join with the Pope in making the consecration. As Sister Lucia has stated: "The responsibility of those bishops is theirs. Because of them God did not refuse to accept the consecration which was made (in 1984) as the one having been requested" (*ibid.*, pages 7–8).

However, it is because this element of collegial union, by "the Holy Father, in union with all the bishops," had in truth been lacking in John Paul II's first consecration in 1982, as we have seen, that he determined to repeat it again so soon afterwards, in 1984. As I have shown above, this deficiency in the 1982 consecration was remedied in every respect in the 1984 consecration. Indeed, in his deep desire to comply with Our Lady, and in his trust in the efficacy of the act of consecration to her Immaculate Heart— "how deeply we feel the need for the consecration of humanity and the world"—it had fallen to him to be the first Pontiff to perform the act in the way required by God. In two important respects John Paul II went considerably further than was implied or expressed in the simple words of Mary's request. In order to underline the solemnity and universality of his consecration in 1984, as Sister Lucia has recognized, the Holy Father greatly enhanced the value of the act, firstly, by performing the consecration outside St. Peter's Basilica in Rome, in front of the statue of Our Lady, which had been brought from Fatima for that purpose; and secondly, by inviting the Orthodox bishops, as well as some Protestant bishops, to unite with him in making the consecration.

Accordingly, on the question of the collegiality of the act of consecration of John Paul II in 1984, we may draw the following conclusions. As regards the Holy Father, what he did perfectly fulfilled the request of Our Lady; As regards the bishops, firstly, a "moral totality of the world's bishops joined the Pope in this collegial consecration," in the words of Alberto Cosme do Amaral, Bishop of Leiria-Fatima, and secondly, although some of the bishops were not united with the Holy Father, the responsibility for that decision was theirs, and God did not on that account refuse to accept the consecration, as Sister Lucia has stated.

The 1984 consecration included Russia

The other issue which has been the cause of considerable confusion in the 1984 consecration, concerns the omission of the specific mention of Russia from the text used by the Holy Father.

In the analysis above, I considered how the Holy Father willingly complied with the request of Our Lady, in a manner that was visible in his thoughts, his words, and his actions, to ensure that his union with the bishops was truly collegial. Our Lady had clearly specified a precise order in which the consecration was to be carried out, and so at this point literal fidelity to the content of the message was required, since here a request from God was being presented by His Mother to the Holy Father, asking him, as Head of the Church, and "in union with all the bishops," to "make the consecration of Russia . . . "

But when it comes to the object of Our Lady's request to the Holy Father, namely, "to make the consecration of Russia to my Immaculate Heart, promising to save it by this means" (*Fatima in Lucia's Own Words*, page 200), it is noticeable that here, by contrast, Our Lady's mission was simply to convey the request for it from God into the hands of the Holy Father, through Sister Lucia, and that no indication was given, either as to what precise form the consecration should take, or when it was to be carried out. The reason for this absence of direction is not difficult to conjecture. Our Lady was calling for a consecration which would "save Russia by this means," as she had said in her communication to Lucia in June 1929, just after the seer had been granted the vision of the Mystery of the Holy Trinity. (In July 1917 the phrase she had used was: "In the end . . . Russia will be converted.") She was requesting an act which derived its force and mission from God, and was designed to intervene, through her Immaculate Heart, in one of the principal nations in the world, for the deliverance of souls that were suffering under the yoke of atheism.

When that vast and deeply Christian country was suddenly overwhelmed by a brutal and militantly atheistic regime, which openly proclaimed its determination to wage war against God throughout the world, just as Our Lady had forewarned in July 1917, the Church was confronted with a problem of unprecedented complexity and sensitivity. The period in question covers perhaps the most turbulent decades in this "difficult and dramatic century," from June 1929, when the request was finally revealed to Lucia, up to the summer of 1981, when John Paul II was recuperating in the hospital from the atheist-inspired attack of May 13. It was then, as we have seen, that the Pope told Bishop Hnilica: "I have come to understand that the only way to save the world from war, to save it from atheism, is the conversion of Russia according to the message of Fatima."

In the absence, therefore, of any specific direction from Heaven, it would appear that God was leaving the Holy Father the discretion to decide both the precise form of the act and the most opportune moment for it to be carried out. This view agrees with the observation of Fr. Messias Coelho, that "the apparitions and their messages are charisms, that is, acts of the Holy Spirit. Their interpretation—to be correct—has to be also an act of the Holy Spirit. He is the Soul of the Church. So the only correct interpretation is that of the Church, and not that of seers." Accordingly, when one looks again at this part of Our Lady's message, it seems that there was nothing in the request of Our Lady to prevent the Holy Father from electing to consecrate the whole world to her Immaculate Heart, with all of humanity in it—thereby including Russia and all its peoples in this act. In the event, as we have seen, that is what John Paul II judged it most appropriate to do.

"The power of this consecration lasts for all time and embraces all individuals, peoples and nations," the Pope stated. In his concern that not one person in the whole world should be omitted, John Paul II repeatedly invoked the consecration on "all individuals, peoples and nations . . . the human race . . . the entire human family of the modern world" and "in a special way . . . those individuals and nations which particularly need thus to be entrusted and consecrated." He recalled and included in his own act the two consecrations which his predecessor, Pius XII, had made to the

Immaculate Heart of Mary: first of all, of the world, on October 31, 1942, and secondly, of all the peoples of Russia, on July 7, 1952. Finally, to ensure that the act itself would be pleasing to God, he stated that "we also entrust to you this very consecration of the world, placing it in your motherly Heart."

All these intentions John Paul II brought into his act of consecration, thereby enlarging the simple request of God for the consecration of Russia, out of the greatness of his heart and the global extent of his vision. Its power should "last for all time and embrace all individuals, peoples and nations," so that there should be revealed "once more in the history of the world, the infinite saving power of the Redemption, the power of merciful Love," which "overcomes every evil that the spirit of darkness is able to awaken, and has in fact awakened in our times, in the heart of man and in his history."

Thus, by including in his consecration, all individuals, all peoples, all nations, and the whole world, it is beyond dispute that Russia, too, was included by the Holy Father. John Paul II's splendidly generous, all-embracing intention, to deliver the whole world, through the power of this consecration, from the evil of the spirit of darkness, of which Russia had had the terrible misfortune to become the embodiment, shines out unmistakably from his act. Moreover, God looks through the form of words into the heart that delivers them, and hence knew perfectly that it was the intention of the Holy Father to include Russia in his act, even if it was not explicitly named. Furthermore, immediately after carrying out the act, the Holy Father told Bishop Amaral of Leiria-Fatima that Russia was included in it. In 1981 John Paul II had already declared his intention to Heaven regarding Russia, in touching language of the heart, when he ordered the construction of a church on the Soviet-Polish border, and placed in it the crowned statue of the Immaculate Heart of Mary which had been given to him by Bishop Hnilica. He had even indicated the exact position he wanted it placed: "with its gaze *directed towards Russia*" (my emphasis). Finally, we now know from Bishop Hnilica that John Paul II had his own reason for carrying out the consecration, from the understanding he had after studying all the Fatima documents, that "the only way to save the world from war, to save it from atheism, is the *conversion of Russia* according to the message of Fatima."

As we have seen, Sister Lucia told the Apostolic Nuncio in March 1984 that Russia was now consecrated, and that, as regards the miracle, "God will keep His word." Now that the moment of hope had at last come, after so many years of waiting and suffering, was the world in consequence going to see the intervention that had been promised by Our Lady? The dramatic and unexpected changes that were to shake the continent of Europe and astonish the whole world, and the moving evidence and testimonies to Mary's discreet yet powerful presence in those changes, form the subject of the next chapter.

3

THE ADVENT
OF
MIKHAIL GORBACHEV

Perestroika and Glasnost

The extraordinary and unexpected turnaround in the internal affairs and destiny of the Soviet Union in the latter part of the 1980s has shaken the countries of the former Red empire like an earthquake, initiating changes in the principal spheres of life that are likely to continue for some time to come. The demise of the first officially atheist state in the world, and thereby, of its militant global ambitions, has also dramatically changed the relations of the former Soviet Union with the superpowers and with the international community in general. These events constitute a major watershed in the history of this century, and are the consequence of the rise to power, in the ranks of the

Soviet Communist Party hierarchy, of the son of a peasant family in the Stavropol region of southern Russia, and one of the few Soviet leaders to have been baptized—Mikhail Gorbachev.

An ambitious and able party official, Mikhail Gorbachev had been a protegé of Yuri Andropov, the KGB chief who had master-minded the Soviet invasion of Hungary in 1956, and who had succeeded Brezhnev as General Secretary of the Communist Party in 1982. After Andropov's death, early in 1984, Gorbachev lost the struggle for power to a rival, Konstantin Chernenko, but a significant sign came in March 1984, the same month that John Paul II effected the consecration of Russia, when he was promoted to head the Foreign Affairs Committee of the Soviet Union. Gorbachev finally became General Secretary after Chernenko's death on March 11, 1985, almost exactly one year after the Pope's act of consecration. Many informed observers agree with the view of the eminent French Catholic, Marcel Clement, Professor of Philosophy in Paris, who stated that "the consecration of 1984 permitted Gorbachev's rise to power in 1985" (30 Days, March 1990, page 10).

At age 54, Mikhail Gorbachev was the youngest Soviet leader since Josef Stalin. We know something of his ideas and plans when he came to power from his speech of resignation just over six years later, on Christmas Day, 1991, in which he openly admitted: "Destiny so ruled that when I found myself at the helm of this state, it already was clear that something

was wrong in this country. We had a lot of everything
. . . however, we were living much worse than people
in the industrialized countries . . . All the half-hearted
reforms, and there have been a lot of them, fell
through. This country was going nowhere. *We had to
change everything radically*. . . . I was also aware that to
embark on reform of this calibre and in a society like
ours was an extremely difficult and even risky under-
taking. But even now, I *am convinced that the democratic
reform that we launched in the spring of 1985 was historically correct"* (my emphasis).

No sooner was Mr. Gorbachev in power than he
set in motion his program of *perestroika* (restructuring)
and *glasnost* (openness), which in a surprisingly short
time was to sweep away the Marxist-Leninist tyranny
that had hitherto held the Soviet Union in its iron grip.
Already by November 1985 he was to meet President
Reagan in Geneva, for the first of eight summits that
were to change the relations between the Soviet Union
and the United States beyond all recognition. In 1986
he formally outlined the principles of perestroika and
glasnost to the Communist Party Congress, and early
in 1987 he began the process of democratization by
giving voters the choice of candidates in local elections. In December 1987 Mr. Gorbachev and President
Reagan signed a treaty to cut their nuclear arsenals,
and a year later he announced a program of sweeping
arms reductions in a speech to the United Nations.

1987 was also the year in which a thaw became
noticeable in Soviet attitudes toward religion. Three

prominent religious personalities visited the country—Mother Teresa of Calcutta, Cardinal Jaime Sin of the Philippines, and Greek Orthodox Patriarch Demetrios of Constantinople, the first Greek Orthodox patriarch to go to Russia in four centuries. The *Literary Gazette*, a most influential periodical in the Soviet Union that was believed to reflect Mr. Gorbachev's views, came to the defense of Christian pilgrims who were flocking to the village of Hrushiv in the Ukraine, where apparitions of Our Lady had been reported.

It was also in this year that the Pope designated the period from the eve of Pentecost 1987 to the feast of the Assumption on August 15 in 1988 as a Marian Year in preparation for the jubilee of the year 2000. By means of a spectacular world-wide television link-up, the Pope opened the Marian Year from the Basilica of St. Mary Major, praying the Rosary for world peace together with tens of thousands of Christians who had gathered in sixteen of the major shrines to Our Lady throughout the world. This must have been one of the greatest live international celebrations of the Rosary that has ever taken place. Twenty-two countries were linked by eighteen satellites to the operational center in London, and seventy-five television networks took part in the program. St. Mary Major is the principal church in honor of Our Lady in Rome. It was rededicated to commemorate the declaration of her Divine Motherhood by the Council of Ephesus in 431, and it enshrines an ancient icon of Mary, known as the *Salus Populi Romani*. When he reached the sanctuary, the

Pope stopped to pray in front of this icon, which is perhaps the most venerated image of the Blessed Virgin in Rome.

In 1988 Mr. Gorbachev was appointed President of the Soviet Union, and in December of that year he stunned the General Assembly of the United Nations, as well as his own General Staff in the Kremlin, by announcing sweeping unilateral cuts in conventional Soviet armed forces. In the same year, Mr. Gorbachev also introduced extensive political changes, with the result that the reformers defeated the hardline Communists the following March (1989) for seats in the new Congress of People's Deputies, in the first parliamentary elections to be held in Soviet history. Two months later Gorbachev was elected President of the new Soviet Parliament. When popular uprisings began in November 1989 against the Communist governments of Eastern Europe, and the Warsaw Pact was dissolved, Mr. Gorbachev refused to intervene to repress the new democratic forces that his own program of reforms had unleashed.

It was during the period 1988–90 that significant changes began to take place in the attitude of the state towards the situation of Christians in the atheist Soviet Union. Canon Michael Bourdeaux, founder and director of Keston College, the center for the study of religion under Communism, is one of the most authoritative observers on this subject, and I am grateful for his permission to reproduce the material which follows from his highly informative book, *Gorbachev, Glasnost and The Gospel* (Hodder & Stoughton, 1990).

In the opinion of Michael Bourdeaux, it was in 1987, or more probably early in 1988, that Mr. Gorbachev decided that "it was time to abandon the old dogma that religion was a retrogressive force, a relic of the past which could have no place in the future ideal Communist society . . . and began to act as though he really did need believers to be in partnership with him in the massive task of rebuilding the moral basis of Soviet society. . . ." Accordingly,

On 29 April 1988 a meeting unprecedented in post-war years took place. The setting was the grandiose Catherine Hall in the Kremlin . . . the firm belief among the Orthodox intelligentsia in Moscow is that the Kremlin instigated the meeting, certainly to the extent of suggesting to the Patriarch that he should make a "request" for it. The published information about it shows clearly that Mr. Gorbachev was setting the agenda. . . . The Patriarch and five attendant Metropolitans must have realized that history was about to unfold before their eyes. Gorbachev's speech was statesman-like, challenging and, within certain limitations, open and honest. He began by admitting the mistakes of the past . . . According to Konstantin Kharchev, chairman of the Council for Religious Affairs, who was present on the government side, Mr. Gorbachev stated that "the overwhelming majority of believers accept the policy of perestroika" and are contributing to economic improvements, to "promoting democracy and glasnost." There would be a tangible reward for this: "A new law on freedom of conscience . . . will reflect the interests of religious organizations." He continued: "Believers are Soviet people, workers, patriots, and they have the full right to express their convictions with dignity. Perestroika, democratization and openness concern them as well—in full measure and without any restrictions. This is especially true of ethics and morals, a domain where universal norms and customs are so helpful for our common cause" . . .

The Patriarch's reply put more emphasis on perestroika than on God. Indeed, He was not mentioned. Pimen pledged the unconditional support of believers for "the architect of perestroika." . . . The Patriarch did not make a single request of the government or of Mr. Gorbachev personally . . .
(Michael Bourdeaux: *Gorbachev, Glasnost and the Gospel*, pages 39, 42–44).

Simply to have shown the Church such recognition was an unprecedented break with the past, although, as the author reveals further on, it was greeted with justifiable skepticism at the time, for after two years the government had not even published a first draft of the proposed new law on freedom of conscience, nor laid down a timetable for its introduction. Michael Bourdeaux's book gives valuable first-hand insight into the state of religion in the Soviet Union during this period, and it will surprise many, for example, to learn that there were thirty million baptisms into the Orthodox Church during the period 1971–88, and that nearly 4,000 students enrolled in Orthodox seminaries in 1989, double the number of the previous year. One of the book's most interesting chapters describes the nationwide celebrations to commemorate the Millennium of Christianity in Russia in 1988. This was announced by the Orthodox Church in June, with the permission of the state, and among those attending were several high-level delegates from the Holy See, led by the Secretary of State, Cardinal Casaroli.

On December 1, 1989 another historic first took place when President Gorbachev met Pope John Paul II at the Vatican. In his address, the Pope said: "Your visit enables us to look with greater confidence to the future of the communities of believers in the Soviet Union . . . the new perspectives which have opened up lead us to the hope that the situation will change . . . and that the law on freedom of conscience, soon to be discussed by the Supreme Soviet, will help to guarantee to all believers the full exercise of the right to religious freedom which, as I have said many times, is the foundation of the other freedoms." The Pope saw the meeting as "a sign of the times that have slowly matured, a sign that is rich in promise."

In his reply, President Gorbachev spoke of their meeting as a "truly extraordinary event," and went on to say: "We had much to discuss. I feel that my thoughts and concerns have been duly appreciated, as

well as my explanations of the problems that now
exist in our country, including problems between the
state and various churches, which we are addressing
in a spirit of democracy and humanism and within the
framework of perestroika. . . . People of many confes-
sions, including Christians, Moslems, Jews, Buddhists
and others, live in the Soviet Union. All of them have
a right to satisfy their spiritual needs. Shortly, a Law
on the Freedom of Conscience will be adopted in our
country. . . ."

Commenting on the historic meeting afterwards,
Cardinal Agostino Casaroli, the Vatican Secretary of
State, observed that it constituted "a substantial turning-point . . . the passage from a very hard winter, and
without hope of spring, to the beginnings of a springtime." The Cardinal said that one of the Vatican's
strongest cards in its decades of dealing with Communist regimes had been the militancy and sufferings of
the Catholics of Eastern Europe, "the religious resistance, many times at the sacrifice of prison and even
death, of these confessors of the Faith." He thought
that Mr. Gorbachev had abandoned the idea of impos-
ing atheism, and added that now there was "even an
appreciation of the values that cooperation with religion can have in the formation of humanity. Peace,
disarmament and political accords are not enough,"
said the Cardinal. He added that above all, the formation of a moral conscience was needed, and it was here
that the Catholic Church especially had a great role to
play, "a role that John Paul II constantly tries to accomplish with vigor," by stressing human and religious rights and the needs of the poor.

Pope John Paul II with Mikhail and Raisa Gorbachev

On March 15, 1990 the Vatican established diplomatic relations with the then Soviet Union, and appointed Archbishop Francesco Colasuonno to be the representative of the Holy See, based in Moscow. Previously, Archbishop Colasuonno had been appointed, on April 19, 1986, as the nuncio with special responsibilities for all the nations of the Eastern bloc. In February 1990, the Communist Party was compelled to surrender its privileged monopoly of political power, and in March Lithuania declared itself independent, to be followed by Latvia and Estonia. Boris Yeltsin, who had been sacked as Moscow Party chief in November 1987 by Mr. Gorbachev, returned to public office in May 1990, when he was elected president of the Russian Parliament.

In 1991, Michael Bourdeaux published in America a revised and updated edition of his book cited above, re-titled as *The Gospel's Triumph over Communism* (Bethany House Publishers, Minneapolis). By his further kind permission, I am able to cite from his new edition the following information about the general new law on religion, which was eventually promulgated in the Soviet Union in September and October 1990.

Prior to this new law, one or two piecemeal changes had been introduced, including the surprisingly liberal law of March 1990, enabling religious organizations to own property. This had overturned one of Lenin's key decrees, but it had not dealt with the question of the billions of rubles' worth of property that had been stolen from the Church in the early days of the Revolution.

The new law itself, Michael Bourdeaux explains, is complicated by the fact that two laws were eventually promulgated, one for all the territories of the USSR, and another, which varied from the former on a number of points, for the territory of the Russian Republic. Bourdeaux writes:

> In most regards, the USSR law is satisfactory if viewed in the context of such international formulations as the UN Declaration on Human Rights and the Helsinki Agreement, while it would not be unfair to categorize the Russian law as "liberal"... both sets of laws abolished over seventy years of repressive Leninist-Stalinist legislation in one sweep . . . Both versions of the law allow freedom of expression for an individual's religious—or indeed atheistic—beliefs . . . Producing religious literature is now legal. No atheist activities are ever to be permitted on church property, while Christian lectures are now frequent on state (formerly atheist) property. . .
>
> Both versions of the new law accept the right of a religious body to establish educational institutions for its own purposes . . . The Russian law (but not that of the USSR) states that citizens may request (state) schools to provide optional teaching by representatives of registered religious associations . . . In practice, head teachers have been welcoming some clergy, including foreigners, into (state) schools in the belief that what they have to say will help fill the moral vacuum created by failed Communist indoctrination. . . .

Both versions of the law now ensure that major religious festivals will be public holidays, and already there has been wide public celebration of both Christmas and Easter.... The Russian law is stronger than its counterpart in guaranteeing citizens against any form of persecution on account of their beliefs . . . No clergyman, in the Russian version, must ever be questioned about what he has heard in the confessional. Both versions make provision for conscientious objection. . . .

The old and widely-hated requirement to register religious associations persists, but in much modified form and mainly to guarantee the body's legal status . . . The Council for Religious Affairs, so widely hated in the bad old days, persists in USSR law, but the Russian version abolishes it. (Michael Bourdeaux: *The Gospel's Triumph Over Communism*, pages 70–74).

Commenting on the events that had been taking place in the Eastern bloc, the Holy Father told Bishop Hnilica, as reported in the March 1990 issue of *30 Days*, that he was convinced they related to the promises of Fatima, and the Korean Catholic weekly of November 11, 1990 carried a similar report: "During the recent synod in Rome, the Korean bishops were invited to lunch with the Pope. In the course of conversation Bishop Angelo Kim, President of the Korean Episcopal Conference, said to the Pope, 'Thanks to you, Poland has been freed from Communism.' John Paul II replied: 'No, not me, but by the works of the Blessed Virgin, in line with her affirmations at Fatima.'"

There are well-informed Catholic commentators who are of the same opinion. For example, Professor Marcel Clement, of the Free Faculty of Comparative Philosophy in Paris, has stated: "What is now happening in the East has such stupefying and unexpected dimensions, and is occurring so rapidly, that one can only say: the hand of God is there. And because there were extraordinary promises made at Fatima, if the hand of God is there, it is because it is in relation to the words of Mary at Fatima. The consecration of 1984 permitted Gorbachev's rise to power in 1985 . . . The present events certainly do not show that the prophecy has been fulfilled, but they do render it credible. Everything will depend on the religious freedom that is granted under the new conditions." Frossard, the French Catholic writer and occasional columnist for *Le Figaro*, when asked for his views, said: "It does not seem at all illogical to me that what is happening in the East should be a consequence of the promises of Fatima. It is evident to me that a kind of miracle is taking place. Moreover, no one can give a purely rational and political explanation for what is taking place." (*30 Days*, March 1990, pages 10, 14)

The pilgrimage to Fatima in May and July 1990 of Cardinal Meisner of Cologne and Cardinal Paskai of Hungary

In May 1990, Cardinal Meisner, who until two years before had been Bishop of Berlin in East Germany, led the first official pilgrimage to Fatima as Archbishop of Cologne, to offer thanksgiving to Our Lady from the faithful of East Germany. In July, Cardinal Paskai of Hungary came on a similar pilgrimage of thanksgiving. Both these eminent prelates spoke eloquently in their homilies of Mary's protection and intervention in their countries during the years of persecution, and I am indebted to Fr. Louis Kondor, SVD, editor and proprietor of the bulletin *Seers of Fatima*, for his kind permission to reproduce the passages cited below, from his issue of May–August 1990.

On May 12, Cardinal Meisner revealed that the Bishop of Fatima had invited him to come to Fatima two years before, while he was still Bishop of Berlin. "Today I come as Archbishop of Cologne. And what has not happened during these two years in Germany and in the whole of Central and Eastern Europe?" In his homily at the concelebrated Mass on May 13, Cardinal Meisner openly expressed his convictions:

> . . . In our ancient Europe, which was formerly the fatherland of Christianity, Jesus Christ is almost unable to appear in public. Mary—and with her likewise the Church—has been relegated to the margins of European society. Portugal, however, received her seventy-three years ago—like John at the Cross—into its home. In Fatima Portugal gave Mary a place and a homeland. Setting out from Fatima, Our Lady could begin her task of bringing Christ again to Europe. In Russia and in other nations of Eastern Europe, faith in Christ was practically forbidden. The peoples of East Europe, who had venerated Mary so much, were unable to give her even a little space because atheism had occupied all

spheres of their lives. Therefore, Mary went forth from Fatima to help the troubled disciples of her Son in the Communist countries of Eastern Europe. Fatima is like the head of a bridge, as it were, which Mary uses to bear Christ to the peoples of the East, for it is He who in reality gives freedom to man. Europe will never forget this opening of the doors to Mary by Portugal. Departing from here, Mary could convert the European states in the east of this continent.

I am here today in Fatima for the first time as Archbishop of Cologne. Previously, I was Bishop of Berlin, and I lived for forty years in a Socialist country. This day in Fatima is a deeply moving one for me. The atheism proposed by the German Democratic Republic until 1989 was a dark cloud under which we had to live. In this sense, we were intimately connected and related to the Christians of the other atheistic countries of Eastern Europe. In the name of Christians from this region of Europe, I would like today to thank Mary who, going out from Fatima, took under her special protection all of Eastern Europe, which was formerly so Christian. And I have come to Fatima to thank the Portuguese people for having received Mary and for having made this work of conversion possible.

The media generally report only the external activity of politicians and of people who have led demonstrations on the streets and in the squares of Eastern European capitals, protesting against atheistic and inhuman systems. But few realize that deep secrets nourish these protests and this resistance. They are ignorant of the basic causes which do not permit the hunger and thirst of men for justice and truth to remain dormant, in spite of all the efforts to instill false hopes and in spite of the promises and threats of Marxism. From outside, nobody could see where the people found the secret reserves of strength to live through those forty years—in Russia, even more than seventy years—in that atheistic and inhuman desert.

Mary was, during those years, an ever-present companion in suffering, and the helper of the persecuted. Just as at the wedding of Cana, she was and is present with men as a Mother with kindly eyes which see what is lacking. She warns the child and gives, today as formerly, the counsel: "Do whatever He tells you!" Therefore men did not follow Karl Marx but Jesus Christ. They did not believe in the Communist Manifesto but in the *Magnificat*. It was not Marx who brought greatness and dignity to men, but Mary. She confesses this in the *Magnificat* in proclaiming: "For the Almighty has done great things for me."

So that the freedom acquired exteriorly may also bring about that men be interiorly free, we direct today our supplication to Mary. Because, if man is liberated from exterior exploitation, he is not yet today freed from himself, in order to find Christ and his mission in the Church and in the world. To seek and find the Lord is the task of Eastern and Western Europe today! Mary sought Christ when she went on pilgrimage to Jerusalem, and she found him in the temple. Would that Mary, today likewise, could accompany Europeans in their search for Christ, and thus with her they will arrive at the Church of her Son.

Therefore we pray to Mary: "And after this our exile, show unto us the blessed fruit of thy womb, Jesus, O clement, O loving, O sweet Virgin Mary!" Amen.

On page 6 of the same issue, Fr. Kondor reported that at the conclusion of the Eucharist, the "Advent 2000 Lamp" was lit and carried in the Adeus farewell procession to the Chapel of the Apparitions, where it was placed near the statue of Our Lady and will remain burning until the third millennium of the Christian era begins. Fr. Kondor also informed his readers, on the same page of this issue, that the Bishop of Leiria-Fatima, Alberto Cosme do Amaral, who holds the maximum responsibility in regard to the Sanctuary of Our Lady of Fatima, stressed the conviction of Cardinal Meisner, President of the pilgrimage, in the following statement:

Everything leads us to think that the consecration requested by Our Lady has been done ... Let us no longer importune the Holy Father, who has done everything that it is possible for him to do. And it is lawful to think that everything which, surprisingly, has happened in Eastern and Central Europe—religious liberty recognized by governments, institution of the sacred hierarchy, respect for the fundamental rights of the human person—can be attributed to the intervention of Our Lady, solicitous Mother of all men and all peoples.

God is ultimately the supreme guide of human history. He alone made history in the person of Jesus Christ. He used Mary. It is permissible to think that all of God's gifts pass through the heart of His and our Mother. In her all graces materialize. But what is important for humanity of this century and the centuries of the future is the fidelity to the message of Fatima, always new and genuine as the Gospel, with which it is identified.

Then, in the silence of our most profound intimacy, each one of us will affirm his *Yes* to the appeals of Our Lady, in silence, in profound silence. They are the appeals of a Mother! And what a Mother!

Later, emphasizing his wish that the faithful should make the statement above as widely known as possible, the Bishop of Leiria-Fatima said: "In what concerns the Consecration, I wish that all possible diffusion be given to the communication I made about Our Lady on May 13, 1990" (reported in *Fatima Family Messenger*, April–June 1991, page 23). Finally, Fr. Kondor concluded the same issue of the Bulletin with a report of the pilgrimage in July of Cardinal Paskai of Hungary, accompanied by five bishops, forty-two priests and about one hundred pilgrims, who came to Fatima to give thanks for the great changes which had occurred. In his homily on July 13, Cardinal Paskai attributed these changes to the special intervention of Our Lady:

> . . . We have come here, then, to welcome Mary's advice and to follow the doctrine of Jesus. We have heard in Fatima the message of Mary, and we shall return to our homes with the firm resolve of wanting to fulfill our Heavenly Mother's request, in penance, in prayer and in the daily recitation of the Rosary. With this spirit of reparation we entrust ourselves and the whole world to her maternal love.
>
> This July pilgrimage has a special significance for the whole of Europe. Sister Lucia, in her memoirs, tells us that, in July, Our Lady asked for reparation so as to avoid another, even worse war. She asked expressly for the consecration of Russia so that it would be converted, for otherwise it would spread its errors throughout the world. However, in the end the Immaculate Heart of Mary will triumph; the Holy Father will make the consecration of Russia, and that country will be converted.
>
> Before our pilgrimage here, profound changes have begun in the countries of Central and Eastern Europe. The events that happened cannot be explained by purely human factors. Politicians who are believers also acknowledge that the hand of God can be seen in these changes. We too are certain that the promise of Our Lady is being fulfilled, and that these changes are the result of her intercession.

Likewise, in my homeland, in Hungary, great transformations are taking place precisely in a tranquil
manner and by peaceful means.

I wish to manifest here, in the Sanctuary of Fatima, my deepest conviction that we are experiencing the intervention of the Most Holy Virgin. Two
years ago we celebrated the 950th anniversary of
the death of Saint Stephen, first King of Hungary.
He was also the first in our history to entrust the
kingdom to Our Lady, shortly before he died. In celebrating this date, the Church in Hungary renewed
this entrusting, and from that very moment, our situation began to improve gradually, and our Church
recovered its liberty. We feel, therefore, the obliga-
tion of showing our gratitude, in this pilgrimage,
for Mary's intercession.

I have come to the Sanctuary of Fatima, accompanied by pilgrims from these countries where historic changes are a fact. Yet I know also that these
alterations rest on fragile bases. I am not referring to
problems of a political and economic order, but
rather in the first place to a religious and moral
fragility. The last four decades have weakened faith
and Christian morals too much, and freedom has
brought with it moral license and secularization
also, things which are opposed to the Christian life.
Besides this, Russia, named by Our Lady in her July
apparitions, is still in a critical condition. Certainly
there also significant changes have taken place, but
it still lacks stability and religious liberty. The Bible

teaches us to observe the "signs of the times." Here also, in Fatima, we note with great joy historic changes. At the same time, we can see the fragile nature of things. Therefore, Mary alerts us decisively towards the necessity of reparation, prayer and especially the praying of the Rosary. In recognizing the signs of the times, we will never tire of requesting, in a spirit of reparation, the intervention of Mary, in these countries and in the whole of Europe.

Virgin Mary, accept our reparation and our prayer. We recommend to you the whole world, Europe, the countries recently liberated and, in a special manner, we entrust Russia to your protection."

Fr. Kondor concluded his report on the Hungarian pilgrimage with the following interesting details. The presence of the Hungarian group was the special event of the July pilgrimages in 1990. On their arrival on the 11th, they began with a solemn concelebrated Mass in the Basilica, where a statue to Saint Stephen, the first King of Hungary, was erected in 1955. On the 12th, they made the Way of the Cross at the Cabeco. All the Station chapels, as well as the final Calvary Chapel of St. Stephen, were built and dedicated in 1964 with offerings donated by Hungarians from all over the world. On the 14th, the whole group took part in a solemn Mass with the nuns of the Carmel of Coimbra, including Sister Lucia, in thanksgiving for the recent transformations that have taken place in their native Hungary. And at the close of their pilgrimage, they solemnly renewed the consecration of all Hungarians to the Immaculate Heart of Mary. Several reporters from Hungarian television accompanied this historic pilgrimage, which was subsequently publicized throughout the country, to the great joy of the Hungarian people.

Shortly before Cardinal Paskai's visit to Fatima, the Hungarian parliament voted by an overwhelming majority to abolish the emblems of Communist rule, and to replace them with the traditional Hungarian coat of arms, which incorporate the famous Crown of St. Stephen.

Homily of Cardinal Korec of Nitra, Slovakia, May 10, 1992

Before concluding this chapter with a look at further changes of an unprecedented nature that were taking place in Eastern Europe in 1990, I briefly move forward in time to 1992, in order to give the text of a homily by His Eminence Cardinal Jan Korec of Nitra, in Slovakia, because of the interesting light it adds to the witness of the two Cardinals from whom I have just quoted. Cardinal Korec recounts how the faithful were able to endure the yoke of atheism in his country, situated in the middle of Central Europe.

The diocese of Nitra was established in the year 880, and is therefore the oldest diocese in Central and Eastern Europe. In February 1990 Pope John Paul II appointed Jan Chrysostom Korec to be the Bishop of

Nitra, and in June 1991 the Holy Father named him a Cardinal. On May 10, 1992 Cardinal Korec came to Fatima and celebrated Mass for the delegates attending the Congress on "Fatima and Peace," and I am indebted to His Eminence for his kind permission to reproduce the text of his homily from that Mass.

Before commencing the Eucharist, the Cardinal made a few opening remarks, in the course of which he stated:

In Slovakia for the last fifty years Fatima has become the heart of the veneration of Mary. In our country many books have been published and numerous articles have been written which speak about the apparitions at Fatima. We have meditated on the message of the Virgin of Fatima in our prayers of the Rosary and in our liturgies. We have a secular institute called "Fatima," as well as an organization called "The Family of the Immaculate Virgin," which is inscribed in the Golden Book of Fatima with its more than one hundred thousand members. It was in a very profound manner that our nation received the promises of Fatima saying that Russia was going to be converted.

Atheism as an official ideology has collapsed. Holy Russia is in the process of rediscovering its Christian roots. The fall of atheism has given freedom to us in Central and Eastern Europe—as the Mother of God had promised at Fatima. Her Immaculate Heart has triumphed. Now we pray to her to help us renew the spiritual life of our people, which has been laid waste over forty long years. We know well that the Mother of God of Fatima is always with us!

During Holy Mass, His Eminence delivered the following homily:

> Dear brothers and sisters!
> The Virgin of Fatima belongs to the entire Church. The whole Church knows her, loves her and strives to keep her message. And thanks to her, the Church experiences great gifts of God.
> The nations of Eastern Europe venerate her, and in a particular manner, we venerate her in Slovakia, a country in the heart of Europe between the Danube and the Tatra mountains. We have known the Virgin of Fatima very well for many decades. We pray her Rosary in our families, in Christian movements and in the churches. With her we give thanks to Him who has done great things for her, "He that is mighty," as she herself says in the Canticle of the *Magnificat*. At the same time we thank the Lord for the great things which have been given to us through her from the moment of the Annunciation until today. He that is mighty has done great things for us...
> Yes, "He that is mighty has done great things to me, and holy is His name." Many centuries ago, when a St. Polycarp or a St. Irenaeus heard or read these words, they understood, in the light of the Old Testament, what was meant by these "great things," what result of the works of God the hymn

of the *Magnificat* was proclaiming. In the course of many centuries in the life of the Church, we have seen how these *magnalia Dei*—these great works of God—have given birth to an unheard of number of other great works of God performed in the lives of great saints, of holy popes and bishops, of fathers and mothers, of young boys and girls, and we have seen how these works have expanded in holy rules and realizations of wisdom and love among the nations! The Annunciation of the coming of Christ was the first and greatest of the great works of God in the New Testament. It was an absolute pinnacle, from which every other action of God on this earth is derived.

Throughout the history of the Church, He that is mighty has poured out His blessings on the entire world up to the present time. It was here at Fatima that God who is powerful and good began to construct a new chain of divine actions for the good of the Church, for the good of us all, for the good of the world. The unheard of subjection of the great people of Russia to atheism had hardly commenced when the Mother of God promised that Russia would be converted, this holy Russia where the veneration of the Virgin was so widespread. The persecution persisted throughout long decades and in 1948 crossed into the world of Eastern Europe, including my own Slovak people situated between the Danube and the Tatra mountains.

The Church lost nearly everything in those countries. Her schools, her publishing houses and all the religious orders and diocesan seminaries

were abolished, and the Christian press was suspended. The bishops were imprisoned, along with
many priests and laity. Several of us Jesuit seminarians were clandestinely ordained priests, and one
of these priests, who is now Monsignor Paul Hnilica, was consecrated bishop. When this was found
out by the police, he had to flee the country, but he
still succeeded in consecrating me bishop after my
superiors had insisted that it should be carried out
clandestinely. This took place on August 24, 1951,
when I was only twenty-seven years old and had
been a priest for scarcely more than a year. It was
also at that moment that I began to lead a life of
persecution: working in factories for twenty-four
years, carrying out clandestine ordinations to the
priesthood and, in 1960, being condemned to
twelve years in prison.

The persecution lasted for forty years in our
country and was very, very hard. But we always
had confidence in the Mother of God, the Virgin of
Fatima. The spiritual movement called "The Family of the Immaculate Virgin" began in our country;
its membership grew rapidly, and today it numbers
tens of thousands of people, among whom are a
great number of the sick and the handicapped.
Their names are written in the Golden Book of Fatima, and today they number more than two hundred thousand members in Slovakia. They have
spread as far as Ukraine, where they have gained
more than one million members. They prayed and
trusted unceasingly, and they have always believed

that the merciful Lord will do great and new things
through the intercession of the Mother of God.

Today we sing the *Magnificat* with a profound
sense of gratitude in our hearts. In the first place
we thank the Lord for His most decisive action in
the history of the entire world, by His arrival in the
person of Jesus Christ, which began to change the
bad condition of the world. The Lord has done
great things. His Son is here, His Mother is with us,
the Church is present, and through Jesus and the
intercession of His Mother there will be more *magnalia Dei,* more great and ever new works of God.

These works will be shown forth not only by
the words of Peter and Paul, or of Irenaeus, but
also by their martyrdom. *Magnalia Dei* will unfold
through Francis of Assisi and Therese of Lisieux,
and also through Fatima. Yet more *magnalia Dei*
will be seen through many lay movements, as well
as in the faithful witness of believers during the
most cruel persecutions of the Church in the twentieth century.

We in Eastern Europe, we have experienced
the meaning of the *magnalia Dei*—the great works
of God in our century and in our nations. We have
lived through one of the most cruel persecutions of
the Church and the rebellion of atheism against
God. We know what it means to live under the
pride of rulers who have only contempt for God
and for His intentions with regard to men, nations
and the world. But we have also lived through this
historic fact: that all of the proud rulers, who were

against God and who persecuted His Church for forty long years, were dethroned and finally disgraced—Hitler, Stalin and others. God displayed His power, exercising His dominion over the tyrannical dictators of this world. Almighty God has accomplished *magnalia Dei* against great tyrants, but He has also given weak believers the strength to resist violence and to keep their faith.

In our country it was the faithful who formed the strongest rampart of resistance against the tyranny of atheism and Communism. In Slovakia, Bishops Vojtassak and Gojdis spent long years in prison without being broken. The latter died in prison because of his fidelity to his Greek Catholic diocese. Hundreds of priests resisted the tyranny, not only in prison but also in their parishes, which had been turned over to atheism. Religious communities that were decimated and dispersed nevertheless succeeded in keeping their spirit. Many of their members suffered in the prisons and concentration camps, up until 1968. Clandestine priests who were members of religious orders also suffered in the prisons. Even though they were forced to work, they consecrated themselves to the apostolate, especially among youth and families.

Lay people who were ready to embrace a life of sacrifice renounced their own careers and consecrated themselves to the lay apostolate in several movements. Some of them remained celibate or founded lay communities. Groups of men and women formed "civil branches" of religious congregations. They were engineers, lawyers, doctors and nurses. They lived as civilians, running high risks. As private individuals who did not marry and raise a family, they were suspected and spied on by the police.

During the persecution God raised up several spiritual initiatives. Young people formed religious circles which took part in pilgrimages, and participated in the religious life of the Marian Year. On one occasion, as many as two hundred thousand pilgrims gathered in Levoca, one of the main pilgrimage towns in Slovakia. And it is in our country, as I said, that "The Family of the Immaculate Virgin" was founded. This is a community of sick and physically handicapped people, founded by a nun who is herself physically handicapped. This family of prayer and sacrifice has grown to an enormous extent (two hundred thousand members), and has spread as far as Ukraine.

In the midst of the atheistic persecution of the Church, through other "works of God," we asked for the grace to know the holy truth about man and his life. Those who, at the beginning, allowed themselves to be drawn toward atheism were deceived by it. Atheism destroyed true culture, the character of man and his conscience; it destroyed education and morality, and created a life of oppression in which there was no freedom. Atheists themselves felt the intolerable nature of such a life.

In the USSR the writer A. A. Fadejeu committed suicide in 1956. Before his death, he wrote in a letter: "I cannot see any reason for continuing to live. The art to which I have consecrated my life is destroyed, annihilated ... The best writers are physically destroyed or perish at the hands of the powerful ... I am escaping from an unclean existence in which futility and lies hurl themselves on man ..." Under atheism men felt that materialism was a futility that was unbearable to the soul: "I live with problems as if I was on top of a volcano," wrote one literary critic in the USSR, and then she added: "The human soul unceasingly searches for God ... Without God one can only live with difficulty. ..."

And it is indeed true that hatred held sway over the whole of one's life. Everyone was afraid of everyone else: the teacher of his pupils, the pupils of their teacher, parents of their children, brother of his brother, one priest of another, officer of fellow officer, and workman of fellow workman. It became the triumph of the parasites of society and the informers ... To have someone imprisoned, it was sufficient to inform the police against him. A Slovak writer, who was banned from the Church about 1958, joined the atheists. A few years later, he asked to be admitted to the Church again and, before his death, he sent me a letter with the following sentence: "My father Bishop! From the very bottom of my heart I recognize that all the authorities who have blasphemed against the apparition of the Divinity have humiliated us ..."

Thus men have witnessed the collapse of their attempt to build a life without God. They have seen that "man cannot live on bread alone..." F. M. Dostoyevsky wrote the following prophetic statement: "If one day man were to attempt, wherever it might be, to build his whole life on atheism, he would produce something so obscure, so blind and inhuman, that the whole edifice would collapse under the weight of human curses..." This statement has been confirmed, first by inhuman Nazism and then by inhuman Communism. The structure has fallen. In order to achieve his so-called full development, man sought to free himself from God. Instead, he has destroyed himself as he has destroyed his culture.

The confirmation of the holy truth about man, that he does not live on bread alone but also on the word of God, the confirmation of the sacred character of the human person who cannot be transformed into a docile animal, and the confirmation of the need for God, for freedom and for the truth which have been manifested in our nations of Eastern Europe—all these things are part of God's victory. They are new *magnalia Dei*, new great works of God, which have been done by Him who is all-powerful and whose name is holy! The *Magnificat* is an avowal. The Blessed Virgin bears witness in this canticle to the whole future of humanity. Her witness is a message for us all. Through her and with her, God has done and God does great things. She became the Mother of His Son, in whom all the nations of the world would be blessed through His

Church. All generations of humanity will rejoice in Mary, Mother of Christ.

St. Ambrose wrote: "May the soul of Mary be in each of us so that she may magnify God! May her heart and her spirit be in us so that we may magnify God for His blessings!" Do I magnify the Lord for the great things which He has done for me in the past, and which He does today in the midst of His Church and through her? And am I full of gratitude for the great things with which we are all filled to overflowing, as well as for myself person-ally?

The Blessed Virgin, while remarkable for her overflowing gifts, at the same time remained a silent servant of God. And the gift which she re-ceived in her Son, she immediately gave to us. She gave Him to the Church. First of all in her heart, and then in deed, under the Cross. From the begin-ning, she thought about the whole of her nation, the world, all of us. From her onwards, God will make all future generations of the world blessed. This is what the Gospel wants to lead us all to be-lieve.

Thus we want to say a profound thank you with all our hearts to the Virgin of Fatima for this gift of freedom, a gift which she promised us. Gathered here around the altar at Fatima, we thank her all together for the glory of her Son, giving thanks to God through the Holy Spirit. Amen.

I return now to consider the evidence of further signs that were taking place in Eastern Europe in

1990, indicating changes of a purely supernatural character which would have been quite unthinkable barely a year or so previously, and of which we began to become aware in the West. I give two very brief examples.

In the summer of 1990 there was a report on the BBC television program, *Newsnight,* which I saw myself, in which Jeremy Paxman took viewers into a factory near Moscow which formerly produced Baby Lenin badges for the indoctrination of Soviet children. Such was the prevailing revulsion against Lenin that demand had almost completely dried up and the factory was threatened with imminent closure. However, at the last minute the factory had been saved because a new market had been found in the production of . . . *crucifixes* and *icons of the Virgin and Child,* for which there was an apparently insatiable demand! Viewers saw both the unwanted sheets of Lenin badges, and the burgeoning supply of the new religious articles. I checked with the producer who verified that the news item was correct. He said he had seen the factory for himself, but had not needed to film in it because Soviet State Television had supplied him with a copy of its own footage.

Later that year, on Saturday October 13, the first religious ceremony since the Revolution in 1917 was held in the Cathedral of the Assumption inside the Kremlin. Previously this cathedral had been used as a museum of atheism. And on the next day, Sunday October 14, the first Orthodox Mass since 1917 was celebrated in St. Basil's Cathedral, located on one side of Moscow's famous Red Square, attended by some members of the Soviet Government. A brief picture of this service was shown on BBC television news the same evening. The next day (October 15), the front page of *The Times* carried a picture of Patriarch Aleksy, the head of the Russian Orthodox Church, together with clergy and faithful, processing with icons and banners outside the cathedral, within sight of the Lenin mausoleum. The Mass was reported to be "in celebration of the Virgin Mary's intercession to alleviate human suffering." The leading article in the same issue of *The Times* informed readers that the number of new parishes permitted by the state had risen from three in 1985 to 2,815 in the first nine months of 1989, and that "the Soviet Union is now in the grip of a titanic religious reformation."

How significant that the first Orthodox Mass to be celebrated in St. Basil's Cathedral since the 1917 Revolution was in honor of the Blessed Virgin's intercession to alleviate human suffering. Here is another sign, and one that perhaps is not altogether surprising, because the traditional veneration of the Russian Orthodox Church for Mary, the Mother of God, is well known. There is a fitting testimony to this in the following passage from Fr. John of Kronstadt, a Russian priest with a reputation for sanctity, who died in 1908:

> Make us conformable to your Son and our God, and to yourself, most holy Virgin, Mother of our Lord, for we bear the name of Christ, your Son, as his members . . . O Sovereign Lady, may we not

call you by that name in vain. Manifest upon us, now and for ever, your holy, living, active sovereignty. Do so, all-merciful Mother of the all-merciful King . . . Who, after the Lord, is like unto Our Lady, our all-merciful, all-succoring and most speedy Mediatrix! Therefore you are highly exalted, Our Lady. Therefore, an unspeakable abundance of grace is given unto you, unutterable boldness and power before the throne of God, and the gift of almighty prayer. Therefore, you are adorned with ineffable holiness and purity. Therefore, the Lord has given to you unprecedented power, so that you might guard, defend, intercede for, cleanse and save us, the inheritance of your Son and God and your own. . . . (From the Kronstadt Diary, *My Life in Christ*).

Another important example of this devotion is evident in the numerous buildings inside the Kremlin itself which testify to Russia's deeply Christian past and the great love of the Russian people for the Blessed Virgin. The Kremlin is a triangular enclosure upon a hill on the north bank of the Moskva river, surrounded by a high wall with five gates. Of these, the most celebrated is the Gate of the Savior, which opens out onto Red Square. It formerly contained a venerated icon of Christ, and everyone who passed through the gate had to remove his hat in reverence. There were several churches, palaces and convents situated inside the Kremlin, as well as other important state buildings. Behind the church and tower of Ivan Veliky (great St. John) with its massive bells, stands the

Cathedral of the Assumption, the place where all the emperors of Russia were crowned, and where all the patriarchs of Moscow used to be buried. To the west lies the Cathedral of the Annunciation, where all the Tsars before Peter the Great were baptized and married. Across a small square is the Cathedral of the Archangel Michael, where used to lie buried all the Tsars of the Rurik and Romanov dynasties, down to Peter the Great. Finally, toward the western end of the Kremlin is the Great Palace, a focus of Moscow's history until after the time of Peter the Great. It was here, as will be seen further on, that Presidents Gorbachev and Yeltsin were interviewed live on American television, following the collapse of the coup.

After witnessing the unprecedented changes that had shaken Central and Eastern Europe in 1990, many observers were left wondering where the whole process was leading. But no one could possibly have foreseen the extraordinary manner of the passing of the USSR, as recounted in the next chapter, that was to take place within the following year.

4

THE PASSING
OF
THE USSR

ON MAY 12, 1991 Pope John Paul II returned to Fatima for the second time . "The pilgrimage this year had a particular purpose: to give thanks for saving the Pope's life on May 13, 1981, exactly ten years ago," stated the Holy Father, in the general audience of May 15, after his return to Rome. *I consider this entire decade to be a free gift, given to me in a special way by Divine Providence ..."* (my emphasis).

At the end of this study I analyze the words addressed to the faithful by the Holy Father on this occasion. Meanwhile, I pause to consider the symbolic significance of a relatively small but by no means unimportant detail concerning the presence of the Vicar of Christ at Fatima. The Pope knelt in silent prayer for almost ten minutes at the feet of the Pilgrim Virgin statue in the Capelinha at the start of the candle-light prayer vigil on May 12. How many people are aware that the richly-bejewelled crown on the head of the statue of Our Lady, which looked down on Pope John Paul II, contains one of the bullets which struck him outside St. Peter's Basilica in Rome?

The symbolic meaning of this gesture is more profound than a simple reference to the person of John Paul II, whose life had been saved by Our Lady. Projected in human terms, the bullet stands for the atheistic totalitarian dictatorship of lies and fear, ruthlessly imposed upon a helpless people by the rule of the gun. Whereas the crown stands for the spiritual sovereignty of the papacy and the Church, God's kingdom upon earth, against which that former regime had vowed such a relentless war. Projected further still, in purely supernatural terms, the presence of the bullet which was intended to assassinate the Vicar of Christ, but is now inside the crown on the head of Mary, Mother of God and Mother of the Church, symbolizes the eternal confrontation between the serpent and the Woman, prophesied in Genesis.

The whole symbolism is so remarkable that it merits deeper reflection. The atheist-inspired attack on the life of the Pope succeeded only in bringing about the exact opposite of its intended object. Indeed, by leading the Pope, as we have seen, to a deep commitment to the message of Fatima and a determination to effect the collegial consecration of Russia to

The statue of Our Lady of Fatima with the crown containing the bullet that struck Pope John Paul II

Mary's Immaculate Heart, the assassination attempt could be said to have served the designs of Divine Providence for the Church. Ten years later, it was the Vicar of Christ, the intended victim of atheist tyranny, who was able to rejoice with the whole Church in thanking Mary for "having guided people to freedom with your motherly affection." And by May 1991, it was Marxist Communism that was already tottering, destined, within a very short time, to hear its own death-knell from the lips of its leaders, in the most public pulpit available. However, as the Holy Father prayed at Our Lady's feet at Fatima in May 1991—and surely we may believe that he knew of the presence of the bullet inside the crown—no one could have foreseen the dramatic culmination that was yet to be played out three months later, in Moscow, in a week that was wholly Mary's—the octave week of the Feast of the Assumption.

The act of placing the bullet inside the crown beautifully exemplifies John Paul II's great faith and trust, that no sin or evil of the world can ever overcome God's love. But there is something more. The bullet was already there when the Holy Father came to honor Our Lady at Fatima in May 1991. This was three months before the collapse of the hardline coup in August, and seven months before the final dissolution of the Soviet Union by President Gorbachev on Christmas Day. Did not this foreshadow the passing of the regime represented by that instrument of death through the victory of the Woman who, in the New Testament dispensation, has been crowned by her Divine Son with the dignity of Queen of Heaven and earth, and under whose foot the head of the serpent is crushed?

Mary's presence in the events of August 19–22, 1991

I pass on now to summarize how the events in Russia of August 19–22, 1991 are connected to Our Lady's Immaculate Heart in a truly special way.

When we reflect on the significance in supernatural terms of the remarkable chain of events that began to unfold after the attempt on the Holy Father's life in 1981, we can see that it must have been in the design of Providence that the momentum of the whole process of change, including the restoration of freedom of worship, finally became irreversible when the attempt to restore the old hardline regime rose and collapsed. This occurred within the Church's liturgical octave of the Feast of the Assumption of Our Lady into Heaven, August 15–22. Here, to those who believe, is an unmistakable sign of Our Lady's intervention, and in fact every day of the duration of the coup recalls some aspect of the devotion to Mary which God wishes to establish in the world.

At Fatima in 1917, August was the only month when Our Lady did not appear to the children on the 13th—because on that day they had been forcibly abducted and put in prison by the Administrator of Ourem. In that month, Our Lady appeared to them instead on the *19th*, not at the Cova da Iria, but at Valinhos, on the hill near the site of the apparitions of the Angel of Portugal in 1916, close to where the Way of the Cross was subsequently erected. The coup was launched against President Gorbachev on the same day, August 19, 1991.

It is also interesting to note that in the Church's liturgical calendar, August 19 is the feast of St. John Eudes. This seventeenth-century saint had consecrated himself to the Blessed Virgin by a vow of perpetual chastity at the age of fourteen, and it was mainly due to him that devotion became widespread to the Most Pure Heart of Mary, as it was then called. St. John Eudes was described by Pope St. Pius X, whose own feast day of August 21 is mentioned below, as "Father, Doctor and Apostle of the liturgical worship of the Sacred Hearts of Jesus and Mary." St. John Eudes was the first to celebrate a Mass and divine office in honor of the Immaculate Heart of Mary, and there is a statue of him in the Basilica at Fatima.

The next day, August 20, is the feast of St. Bernard, of whom Bossuet said, "he had a special devotion to the Blessed Virgin, and there is no one who speaks more sublimely of the Queen of Heaven." But on August 20, 1991, apart from the Moscow coup, another event of great significance was taking place in Central Europe. It was the last day of Pope John Paul II's visit to Hungary, and for the first time since their liberation from the Communist yoke two years previously, people had gathered in Heroes' Square, the largest open space in Budapest, to celebrate the feast of St. Stephen, the first king of Hungary. Stephen consecrated Hungary to Our Lady as its Queen and Patroness before he died on August 15, 1038. His feast is celebrated in Hungary on August 20, the day when his relics were transferred to Budapest. It was only three years before, in 1988, on the 950th anniversary of St. Stephen's death, that the Church was permitted to celebrate his feast with people outside as well as inside the church. Astonishingly, the regime had even permitted and assisted with the display of the saint's relics throughout the country. On that occasion, in the presence of an enormous crowd, Cardinal Paskai, together with all the bishops of Hungary, consecrated their country again to Our Lady, outside St. Stephen's Basilica in Budapest.

In 1989 Hungary was liberated from the Communist yoke, the Iron Curtain was torn apart, and thousands of East Germans escaped to Hungary and then to the West. As we have seen, Cardinal Laszlo Paskai, Primate of Hungary, went to Fatima on a pilgrimage of thanksgiving in July 1990 and publicly voiced his deeply-held conviction that "we are experiencing the intervention of the Most Holy Virgin." But now, a year after that, on the last day of the Pope's visit, August 20, 1991, the whole country was gripped by a terrible shock wave of fear that the Moscow coup would lead to the return of brutal tyranny and reprisals in their country. I was told this by a Hungarian priest who was there at the time. It was known that former Hungarian Communists were already preparing a retaliatory coup of their own.

The Holy Father presided at the Solemn Mass, and at its conclusion, together with all the country's bishops, he renewed the consecration of Hungary to Our Lady, asking her to come to the aid of the nation and save it from peril. After the consecration, the Holy Father asked God to spare the Soviet Union further tragedies, and recalled his two meetings with President Gorbachev in the following impromptu words: "I especially appreciated the sincere desire that led him and the noble inspiration that guided him in promoting human rights and dignity ... The process he began must not be broken off!" (*L'Osservatore Romano*, English edition, September 9, 1991).

The coup collapsed the next day, August 21st, about 6:30 pm, that is, already within the first vespers of the feast of the Queenship of Mary on the following day, and its ending could not have been more complete or peaceful: the eight-man state emergency committee simply announced that it no longer existed. A few hours later, about three o'clock in the morning of August 22nd, President Gorbachev arrived back in Moscow with his family, safe but visibly shaken. However, instead of acknowledging the role of Boris Yeltsin and the crowds outside the Russian Parliament Building in helping to defeat the coup and thereby effectively saving his own life, he went back to his office in the Kremlin and stated, apparently in sincere but misguided belief: "I will fight to the end for the renewal of the Communist Party." With those words, he sealed his own fate, for when he went to address the deputies of the Russian Parliament on the 23rd, their leader, Boris Yeltsin, compelled him to read out the minutes of the coup's leaders, which proved that his own ministers had acceded to their demands. On the 24th, President Gorbachev resigned as leader of the

Communist Party and banned it from all state bodies. All his ministers were sacked, fourteen were later charged with high treason, and the KGB was purged.

To return to the liturgical cycle within which all these events were taking place, the presence of Our Lady is again evident on August 21, for that was the feast day of St. Pius X, the great Pope at the beginning of this century who had approved the use of the scapular of the Sacred Hearts of Jesus and Mary. In Ireland August 21 is also celebrated as the feast of Our Lady of Knock.

It is a fact that the final dissolution of Marxism and the Communist party was set in motion on August 22, which is so significant because that is the day in the Church's calendar on which was formerly celebrated the feast of the Immaculate Heart of Mary. The feast of August 22 has recently been changed to the Queenship of Mary, and the feast of the Immaculate Heart of Mary has been moved beside the feast of the Sacred Heart of Jesus in June. This is in keeping with the desire of Our Lord expressed to Lucia, that the Church put the devotion to Mary's Immaculate Heart beside the devotion to His Sacred Heart.

It is instructive at this point to recall how the feast of the Immaculate Heart of Mary came to be instituted on August 22. As we have seen, Pius XII, the Pope of Fatima, made the first consecration of the Church and the whole world to the Immaculate Heart of Mary on October 31, 1942. That was the twenty-fifth jubilee year of the apparitions, and also of his own episcopal consecration. In order to underline its relationship with Fatima, the Pope decided to make the consecration in the course of a radio broadcast to the Portuguese nation, which he delivered on the closing day of the jubilee ceremonies. However, as this first consecration was pronounced in Portuguese, and therefore was likely to pass largely unnoticed, Pius XII repeated the act in St Peter's Basilica on December 8, 1942, the Feast of the Immaculate Conception, in order to underline its significance for the whole Church.

"In order to preserve the memory of this consecration," states the decree of institution issued May 4, 1944, "he (Pius XII) ordered that the 22nd of August, Octave day of the Assumption, should be observed throughout the Church as the feast of the Immaculate Heart of Mary, a Double of the Second Class. The purpose of the feast is to obtain, through the help of the Blessed Mother of God, peace for all nations, freedom for the Church of Christ, conversion for sinners; and for the faithful, grace to grow stronger in their love of purity and the practice of virtue."

Looking back over the extraordinary chain of events that has unfolded from March 25, 1984 to August 22, 1991, we can now see that this period begins and ends with the consecrations to the Immaculate Heart of Mary by two of the great Marian Popes of this century. Following the act carried out by John Paul II on March 25, 1984, in fulfillment of Our Lady's request, it is indeed a remarkable confirmation of her promised intervention that the whole process of change in Central and Eastern Europe finally became irreversible on August 22, 1991, the date of the feast instituted by Pius XII to commemorate the first consecration of the world to Mary's Immaculate Heart.

The most significant of the numerous changes which have taken place in this period, and the one which clearly reveals the efficacious power of the consecration to Mary's Immaculate Heart, is the unexpected collapse of the totalitarian, atheistic ideology embodied in the regime of the former Soviet Union. This has led to the end of the campaign of violent repression and persecution directed against the Church by the Communist Party's militant wing, and the concurrent restoration of the Church's freedom to pursue her divinely appointed mission in the world. In this astonishing reversal, and in the peaceful manner in which it was brought about from within, one can see the hand of God through the intervention of Mary, and the outright accomplishment of one of the principal purposes for which Pius XII instituted this feast.

In regard to the other primary purpose of the feast, to obtain peace for all nations, while this is still a long way from becoming a reality, nevertheless during this same period of change unprecedented initiatives have been taken by the superpowers. The previous cold war confrontational deadlock has been broken, international tension has been lessened, and considerable progress has been made in mutual arms reduction. All this is a further consequence of the demise of the totalitarian atheistic Marxist-Leninist principles on which the Soviet state was founded—described by

Our Lady as "the errors of Russia" in July 1917. For
the collapse of the global threat posed by the ideological ambitions of the former Soviet regime has *ipso facto*
removed one of the chief causes of the devastating
wars of this century, wars that have even led to the an-
nihilation of various nations, exactly as Our Lady
prophesied.

Finally, when one considers the vast arsenal of
arms possessed by the former Soviet Union, and the
equally huge numbers of men in their armed forces, it
is certainly astonishing that the breakup of the former
superpower and its transition to democratic government has so far been accomplished peacefully and
with little bloodshed.

The coup aftermath and the collapse of the Soviet Union

Following the collapse of the coup, the two most
powerful men in the Soviet Union were asked to give
their views on the recent events, on a television interview transmitted live to the United States. When one
reflects on the violent manner in which a number of
totalitarian dictatorships, Communist and Fascist,
have come to an end in the course of this century, here
is another remarkable testimony of how Mary was
bringing about the process of transition and change of
heart that was sweeping the whole Soviet Union
peacefully from within. Sitting in gilded armchairs in
the Kremlin's St. George's Hall, President Yeltsin
openly confessed: "This experiment was a tragedy for

our people and it was too bad that it happened on our territory." President Gorbachev's views were even more explicit: "The historical experience we have accumulated has allowed us to . . . say in a decisive fashion that the model has failed. And I believe this is a lesson not only for our people but for all people." (*Daily Telegraph*, September 7, 1991, page 9. *New York Times*, same date).

President Yeltsin himself has made no secret of his own change of heart with regard to religion. In the course of an interview published in *Izvestia*, the Moscow-based, government-owned newspaper, and quoted on page 11 of *The Irish Catholic* of October 24, 1991, he stated:

"I am baptized. My name and date of birth, as was the rule, are written in the baptismal registry. Later, in the course of a disproportionately ideological formation at school and in the university, I constantly heard, read, and—why hide it—felt and shared the most insulting opinions concerning the Church and religion. This education was gravely wrong and seriously unjust, as was the classification of persons into believers and non-believers, a distinction which today is somewhat blurred. Having said this, I have the greatest respect for the Orthodox Church, for its history, for its contribution to Russian spiritual life, for its moral teachings, its tradition of mercy and charity. Today, the Church is moving ahead in these areas and our duty is, in turn, to re-establish the rights of the Church. A religious service lasting four hours bores neither me nor my wife. And often, when I leave a church, I feel that something new, something luminous, has come into me."

As details of the coup began to emerge, *The Universe* of September 29, 1991 reported that it was a radio station belonging to the Catholic Radio and Television Network, based in Belgium, which helped President Yeltsin to foil the hardliners' plot. The radio station's equipment was in a Moscow warehouse waiting for final clearance before it could start broadcasting. It was smuggled into the Russian Parliament building, concealed in a truck under a load of fruit and vegetables, just as Mr. Yeltsin arrived, after reportedly escaping arrest by the KGB at his home. President Yeltsin was then able to go on the air and ask citizens to rally outside the Parliament building in order to resist the coup. The station kept on the air throughout the crisis, and has continued broadcasting Christian programs eight hours a week ever since—from the top floor of the Russian Parliament building. As a gesture of thanks, the Russian President allowed a Mass from Fatima to be shown live on television in Moscow, on the occasion of the first pilgrimage to visit the shrine from Russia. This historic event is fully described in the next chapter, but meanwhile it remains to recount the most important of the events precipitated by the collapse of the coup. These events culminated in the resignation of President Gorbachev on Christmas Day and the last session of the Supreme Soviet, which met to dissolve itself the next day.

On November 7, as reported in the *Daily Telegraph*, the Bolshevik revolution was for the first time not commemorated with the customary military parade through Red Square. Instead, the Orthodox Church led a procession to mourn the victims of Communism, outside the KGB's old Lubyanka headquarters. On the same day, by popular demand, Russian television repeated the broadcast of the first pilgrimage to go to Fatima from Moscow, which had been shown live on October 13. November 7 was also the day that the city of Leningrad changed its name back to St. Petersburg, and during that week the grand nephew of the last Czar, Grand Duke Vladimir Kirillovich, head of the House of Romanov and now aged 74, visited the city and set foot on Russian soil for the first time in his life.

On December 8, President Yeltsin of Russia and the leaders of Ukraine and Byelorussia announced in Minsk that they had signed an agreement setting up a commonwealth. Here again one discerns the presence of Mary at an important moment in the process of change, for it was on that day, the Feast of the Immaculate Conception, that the death of the old Soviet Union became a foregone conclusion. Surprised by the sudden accord, eight of the nine remaining republics hastily applied to join as charter members, and this led to the Commonwealth of Independent States that was founded at Alma Ata thirteen days later, as we shall see below. Meanwhile, already on December 8, the three founding members of the Commonwealth saw fit to pronounce the Soviet Union dead.

On December 20, the sixteen NATO foreign ministers, attending the first meeting in Brussels of the

North Atlantic Co-operation Council, were taken by surprise when a letter was read out from President Yeltsin, raising the question of Russia's membership in NATO, "as a long-term political aim." This proposal came after decades of antagonism between the Soviet bloc and NATO, and the Russian President went on to say that the new Commonwealth of Independent States, which the former republics of the Soviet Union were in the course of setting up, wanted to help to build "a reliable system of collective security in Europe," which would also include the participation of the United States and Canada, the non-European NATO members.

Mr. Hurd, the British Foreign Secretary, was careful not to rule out eventual Russian membership, but the proposal was perhaps most aptly summarized by Mr. Eyskens, the Belgian Foreign Minister, when he commented: "This is not a reversal of history. It is history being turned inside out."

December 21 saw the effective dissolution of the Soviet Union, when eleven of the fifteen former Soviet republics, meeting in the Kazakh capital of Alma Ata, founded the Commonwealth of Independent States that had been proposed by Yeltsin on December 8. Georgia did not sign but sent observers. Also missing were the three Baltic republics of Lithuania, Latvia and Estonia, whose independence had been recognized by the Supreme Soviet on September 6.

The final act in the whole immense drama was reserved for Christmas Day, and I reflect below on the supernatural significance of that particular day, when

the Church celebrates the birth of Jesus, the divine Son
of the ever-Virgin Mary. For it was on Christmas Day
that Mikhail Gorbachev chose to announce his resignation. The following extracts are taken from his television address to the whole nation, and the speech is
remarkable for its honest and open admission of the
deficiencies of the system that Gorbachev had sought
to reform.

"Due to the situation that has evolved as a result of the formation of the Commonwealth of Independent States, I hereby discontinue my activities
as President of the USSR . . . Destiny so ruled that,
when I found myself at the helm of this state, it already was clear that something was wrong . . . we
were living much worse than people in the industrialized countries . . . Doomed to cater to ideology,
and carry the onerous burden of the arms race, the
country found itself at breaking-point . . . We had to
change everything radically . . . I am convinced that
the democratic reform we launched in the spring of
1985 was historically correct. This society has acquired freedom. It has been freed politically and
spiritually, and this is the most important achievement that we have yet to fully come to grips with ...
The totalitarian system has been eliminated. Free
elections have become a reality. Free press, freedom
of worship, representative legislatures and a multi-
party system have all become reality. Human rights
are being treated as the supreme principle. We are
now living in a new world. An end has been put to

the cold war and to the arms race, as well as to the mad militarization of the country, which had crippled our economy, public attitudes and morals. . . .

All this change has caused a lot of strain, and took place in the context of a fierce struggle against the background of increasing resistance by the reactionary forces, from both the Party and State structures, and the economic elite, as well as our habits, ideological bias, the sponging attitudes . . . I consider it vitally important to preserve the democratic achievements which have been attained in the past few years. We have paid with all our history and tragic experience for these democratic achievements and they are not to be abandoned, whatever the circumstances. Otherwise, all our hopes for the best will be buried. . . .

I am very much concerned as I am leaving this post . . . (but) I am positive that, sooner or later, some day, our common efforts will bear fruit and our nations will live in a prosperous, democratic society. I wish everyone all the best."

That evening the hammer and sickle flag of the former Soviet Union was lowered from the flagstaff above the Kremlin building, and the white, blue and red tricolor of Russia was raised in its place. The same ceremony was repeated in former Soviet embassies around the world. Also on Christmas Day, the Russian Parliament voted to change the republic's formal name from the Russian Soviet Federative Socialist Republic to the Russian Federation, abbreviated simply as Russia.

Finally, on December 26, a handful of people's deputies turned up to go through the formality of voting the dissolution of the Parliament of the Supreme Soviet. With that, the USSR was no more.

It is astonishing to recall the major transformations that have transpired in barely seven years since Pope John Paul II's consecration of Russia in March 1984, and in just over ten years from the attempt on his life in May 1981. In that brief passage of time, the vast Union of Soviet Socialist Republics, a totalitarian dictatorship established and maintained by force, introduced due constitutional and democratic processes which ended up by decreeing the USSR itself out of existence. The Communist Party of the Soviet Union was banned by its own General Secretary for the open complicity of its highest officials in the failed coup against the head of state, despite his desire to fight to the end to renew it. The very instigators of the August 1991 coup, who had sought to abort the processes of change, are to be prosecuted for high treason. The doctrines of Marx and Lenin, on which the first officially atheist state in the world erected a vast monolithic and totalitarian structure, maintained by systematic subversion, indoctrination, violent repression and aggression, have been officially discredited and rejected. The atheistic persecution of God and the Church, the principle which animated the whole system, has ceased, and freedom has been restored to the Church to pursue her divinely appointed mission.

Does history record any comparable instance of how such a tyrannical regime, so powerful that it threatened the peace and stability of the whole world, ended by turning about on itself, publicly avowing its own shortcomings and seeking to reform them, and finally permitting itself to be constitutionally and democratically voted out of existence? Such an example must be without precedent. Indeed, this century alone has seen numerous examples to the contrary, of totalitarian dictatorships that have ended by the same violent means which they used to keep themselves in power.

But then, does history also record any example to compare with the promise given to mankind at Fatima in 1917 by Mary, the Virgin Mother of God, to intervene so powerfully in the destiny of a nation, as we may believe she has done in Russia, when once her requests were complied with?

As I have said, there is a symbolic significance, in supernatural terms, in the fact that Mr. Gorbachev chose to step down from the Presidency of the USSR on Christmas Day. We have noted that the two previous key turning points in the cycle of events that had overtaken the Soviet Union—the attempt on the life of Pope John Paul II in May 1981, and the attempted coup against President Gorbachev in August 1991—both fell on important feasts of Mary in the Church's calendar. They denoted her intervention to prepare for the return of her Divine Son to the public life of the peoples of Russia.

Since Mary's work of preparation had now been completed, it could not have been more fitting that the conclusion of the third and final turning point in the whole process of transformation was destined to occur, not on a feast of Mary, but on the feast of the Nativity of her Divine Son. For on that day the last remaining vestige was removed of the first official atheist state in the world, and Christ was now free to appear again in Russia and to resume His presence and His mission among the people, unopposed by any organs of the state. Just as the most pure womb of the Virgin Mary was the vessel chosen by God for the birth of His Son in Bethlehem, in order to deliver mankind from the darkness of sin and establish His Church upon earth, so in our century the Immaculate Heart of the Virgin of Fatima was the means chosen by God to deliver the peoples of Russia from the bondage of atheism and to restore the presence of Christ in society.

Now that the long-awaited liberation of the Church in Russia and Central and Eastern Europe has come to pass, through the intervention of Our Lady of Fatima, it is appropriate to return there and hear, in the next chapter, an account of the first pilgrimage ever to come to Fatima from Moscow, in October 1991, and a report of how the ceremonies on that occasion came to be transmitted on a live television broadcast direct from the shrine to Moscow.

But before we go to Fatima, let us hear, as a postscript to this extraordinary chapter in European history, the verdict which Mr. Gorbachev himself did not hesitate to proclaim in public on the role of the Pope in bringing about the changes in the former USSR.

Mikhail Gorbachev publicly acknowledges the Pope's role

As reported in the British daily, *The Independent* for March 3, 1992, Mr. Gorbachev has begun to write a regular column in the prominent Italian journal, *La Stampa* of Turin, and in the issue for that day he publicly thanked the Pope for the crucial role John Paul II had played in bringing about the changes in the Soviet Union. When we consider that it was these changes that brought about the demise of the USSR, and with it the extinction of Mr. Gorbachev's own office as President, then once again we are impelled to seek an explanation for this remarkable testimony of recognition in the mysterious interaction of a power other than human.

This view is borne out, firstly, by the ex-President's disclosure of the deep sympathy and understanding that exists between himself and the Pope, and secondly, by some of the Pope's own comments upon reading Mr. Gorbachev's article.

According to *The Independent*, the intense exchange of letters between the two men, to which Mr. Gorbachev refers in his article, may have begun in 1988, when the Pope sent ten cardinals to Moscow to attend the 1,000th anniversary of Russia's conversion to Christianity. The delegation was led by the then Vatican Secretary of State, Cardinal Casaroli, who had taken with him a letter from the Pope, the contents of which have never been made public.

By kind permission of *La Stampa*, I here reproduce the entire text of Mr. Gorbachev's article, published on March 3, 1992.

In recent years I have had an intense exchange of letters with Pope John Paul II, after our meeting in the Vatican in December 1989. And I certainly believe that this dialogue will continue. Between us there is a deep feeling of sympathy and understanding, which we express in each message. But I think I can say that, above all, we have the will to complete and carry forward something which we have created together. For my part, I, for one, want to use every opportunity to continue to work with the Pope, and I am sure that our shared commitment will always remain important to me.

It is not easy to describe the type of understanding that exists between me and Pope Wojtyla, because in a relationship of this kind, enormous importance must be given to an instinctive, perhaps intuitive, and certainly personal element. To put it simply, I can say that my contact with him has made me realize and understand the role of the Pope in the creation of that which later would be called "new political thought." I don't have the slightest difficulty in admitting that I was in accord with many ideas in his discourses. That confirms the understanding, the closeness, which I just mentioned; these ideas were very similar to our ideas.

In the thought of this Pope, I have always appreciated above all the spiritual content, the endeavor to contribute to the creation of a new civilization in the world. In addition to that, John Paul II is not only Pope in Rome, but he is also a Slav, and this fact has certainly contributed to our mutual understanding. But I remain convinced that the spiritual agreement which exists between us represents something larger than our shared Slavic heritage.

Today it is possible to say that everything that happened in Eastern Europe during these last few years would not have been possible without the presence of this Pope, without the leading role, even the political role, that he was able to play on the world scene.

I believe that also important in our new relations with the Vatican are the forward steps that we took here in Moscow with respect to religion. Among other measures, we grasped the necessity of establishing a normal system of relations between the Orthodox and the Roman Catholic Churches, and this has certainly contributed to improving the relations between our country and the Vatican. But above all, perestroika also made its way into the sphere of religion, in a change that culminated in the approval of the law on freedom of conscience.

In this way we re-established the rights of the Orthodox Church in Russia, which had been battered during the years of Stalinism. But at the same time we also recognized the role of other religions in our society—keep in mind that in our country there are also one hundred different faiths. Today I feel I can say that this was a process of liberalization that has a strong moral significance for all citizens, believers and non-believers.

In any case, beyond what we were able to accomplish in this country, I remain convinced of the importance of Pope John Paul's actions in this period. I have already underlined his great spiritual qualities. But I have to add that in our meeting in Rome two years ago I was also very much struck by him as a human being. In short, this is an exceptional individual; I don't want to exaggerate, but I felt something unusual, as though from this person emanated an energy that inspired a deep sense of trust in him.

And today as well, even after the profound change that has taken place in Europe, Pope John Paul will have a leading political role. In fact, we are in a very delicate state of transition, in which the human being, the person, can and should have a really decisive weight in society. Anything that can serve to strengthen the conscience of humanity, the human spirit, is more important now than ever before. (Copyright 1992 by *Editrice La Stampa, S.p.A.,* Turin, Italy. Parts of this article also appeared in *The New York Times,* March 9, 1992.)

At Mr. Gorbachev's request, *La Stampa* personally delivered the text of his article to the Pope, and by the editor's further kind permission, I am able to reproduce the report which was published the next day, March 4, of the private audience granted to *La Stampa*

by the Pope in the Vatican on that occasion. As will be
seen, while the whole of this text is important in helping us to understand the relationship of the two key
personalities at the center of the recent events in Europe, the Pope made two statements in the course of
this audience which are especially noteworthy in relation to the present study, and on which I offer the following brief comments.

In the first place John Paul II throws a revealing
light on the former President's personal attitude to religion and spiritual values, when he says that Mr. Gorbachev "does not profess to be a believer, but with me
I recall he spoke of the great importance of prayer and
of the inner side of man's life." We learn from this observation, and from his own appreciation of the
human and spiritual qualities of the Pope, that even if
Mr. Gorbachev is not apparently a believer, at the least
he is open to some of the deepest spiritual values in-
culcated by Christianity. This attitude may indeed
seem to represent a contradiction, coming from the
man who at the time was General Secretary of the
Communist Party of the Soviet Union. At the same
time it helps one to understand how Mr. Gorbachev
could be convinced that "we had to change everything radically," and how he could claim that his most
important achievement was to have freed society politically and spiritually, as he stated in his speech of
resignation on Christmas Day 1991. For it is evident
that a man who so esteemed prayer and the world of
the spirit could have little or no sympathy with militant atheism, the ideology to which he was doomed to

cater when he found himself at the helm of the Soviet state, as he put it.

Secondly, twice during this audience the Pope unequivocally proclaims his belief that it was Providence which had prepared the meeting between himself and President Gorbachev in December 1989. In two separate references, and with distinct emphasis, the Pope states, "I know . . ." and then "I truly believe that our meeting has been prepared by Divine Providence."

The underlying providential disposition that may be discerned through the remarkable concurrence of key events and dates is one of the principal themes of this study; and here, at one of those key moments, the Pope himself firmly and openly proclaims the reality of this divine interaction in human affairs. Indeed, in his previous reference to the role of Providence, quoted earlier in this chapter, John Paul II seemed to extend this concept when he stated, on his return to Rome from Fatima on May 15, 1991: "I consider this entire decade to be a free gift, given to me in a special way by Divine Providence . . ."

Accordingly, as the role of Providence forms an important aspect of this study, before going on to give the complete report of the Pope's audience, it is appropriate briefly to recall the teaching of the Church on this subject.

The Catholic Encyclopedia (1911 edition, volume 12, page 510) defines Providence as "God Himself considered in that act by which in His wisdom He so orders all events within the universe that the end for which it

was created may be realized. That end is that all creatures should manifest the glory of God, and in particular that man should glorify Him . . . God preserves
the universe in being; He acts in and with every creature in each and all of its activities. In spite of sin,
which is due to the willful perversion of human liberty, acting with the concurrence but contrary to the
purpose and intention of God, and in spite of evil
which is the consequence of sin, He directs all, even
evil and sin itself, to the final end for which the universe was created. All these operations on God's part,
with the exception of creation, are attributed in
Catholic theology to Divine Providence."

Fr. Reginald Garrigou-Lagrange, one of the most
eminent Dominican theologians of this century, sums
it up admirably when he says: "All things are con-
trolled by Providence; the least circumstance, however insignificant, is in its hands. With Providence
there is no such thing as chance" (*Providence*, Herder,
1947, page 262).

What follows is the complete text of the audience
which the Holy Father granted to *La Stampa*, as reported in the issue of March 4, 1992.

"These words are sincere," says the Pope, "and
they confirm what I have always thought about
Gorbachev: he is a man of integrity." The Pope lifts
his eyes up from the pages he has been reading, but
he keeps his finger on the phrase that has struck
him, as if not to lose the meaning of a deeply felt
emotion.

Before him, on a bare table, lies the article written by Mr. Mikhail Sergeivich Gorbachev. The Pope reads it first in Cyrillic, and then in the Italian translation.

The Pope reads the text slowly and in silence. Only at a certain point does he lift his eyes, touched by Mr. Gorbachev's words which reveal a mutual spiritual understanding produced at their first meeting—a relationship that was "instinctive, or perhaps intuitive, and certainly personal" between two men who represent worlds so distant from one another.

"It's true," says the Pope, "there was something instinctive between us, as if we had already known each other. And I know why that was: our meeting had been prepared by Providence."

It was Mr. Gorbachev in Moscow who asked *La Stampa* to deliver the text personally to the Pope, "as a token of my esteem and as a measure of my friendship." That text, which was published yesterday in *La Stampa* and in other newspapers throughout the world, was now in the hands of the Pope. And just as Mr. Gorbachev was aware of the political importance of his assessment of the Pope as a linchpin and initiator of the democratic revolution in the East, so too the Pope paid homage to the man of perestroika. The conversation *La Stampa* had with the Pope in the Vatican—during a private audience in the presence of Dr. Joachim Navarro-Vals, director of the Vatican Press Office—is testimony to the special relationship between the Pope and Mr. Gorbachev, as evidenced by his account of their first meeting in Rome and in the anticipation of the Pope's visit to Moscow. It is also an opportunity to hear the Pope's evaluation of the events that have shaken the Soviet Union and Eastern Europe, seven months after the Moscow coup, wih Mr. Boris Yeltsin now the new leader of the Kremlin.

"I have a strong and distinct recollection of my meeting with Mikhail Gorbachev when he paid a visit here," the Pope said. "I believe he is a man of integrity, committed to principles and very rich in spiritual terms—a charismatic man, who has had a decisive influence on the events in Eastern Europe. He does not profess to be a believer, but with me I recall he spoke of the great importance of prayer and of the inner side of man's life. I truly believe that our meeting was prepared by Providence."

For Mr. Gorbachev it was history and geography that determined the particular conditions enabling the Pope and the Kremlin to come to a mutual understanding at the end of the century. "It's true," the Pope said, "just as he wrote in his article, Gorbachev spoke to me with human warmth and in a kindred way about the 'Slavic Pope.' He said he was happy to find here in the Vatican a pontiff who was a Slav like him and, for that reason, able to understand better the problems of the world.

"I replied by reminding him, smilingly, that I am indeed a Slav, but a western one. He said in turn that that did not matter. It is not a matter of chance that the Pope has chosen to nominate Saints Cyril and Methodius as fellow patron saints of Europe. They represent the point at which the Slavic identity and the Latin identity intersect."

But in Mr. Gorbachev's assessment of the Pope there is not only testimony as to the personal, spiritual and cultural understanding between the two men. For the first time, publicly from Moscow, the Vatican received open acknowledgement of the historic importance of this pontificate for its direct influence on the liberation of the East.

"I read what Gorbachev had to say about the Pope's role in the events which have changed Eastern Europe in these past few years, and I am certain that he sincerely believes those things. But when the European Synod of Bishops wanted to emphasize in their final document this specific role of the Pope, I asked them not to do it. It is the Church, and not the Pope, that has counted in this process. If something can be ascribed to the Pope, it is the fruit of his devotion—his devotion to Christ and to mankind."

The Pope appears to be convinced that the West must be prepared to come fully to terms with the democratic revolution in Eastern Europe, in order to understand its root cause. "There may be those who do not like Gorbachev's assessment. But those events must be evaluated fully and in depth, and the real causes of certain phenomena have yet to be clarified.

"For example, there are those, like Popper, who are convinced that economic difficulties were the source of the crisis of the Communist systems of

Eastern Europe. And of course this element was present and had a certain effect. But we must not forget something very important: there was not simply a crisis of Communism, but there was also a perestroika. And *perestroika* means, among other things, also conversion."

For the Pope this has a great and immediate significance. "This means that in the crisis and breakdown, in the upheaval which took place and is in progress, there is a spiritual element—an inner change. Moreover, that is as it must be, and it could be no other way. Man is made of two elements; an exclusively spiritual interpretation of the events in the East would be mistaken, and just as mistaken would be a solely material one, incapable as it is of looking beyond the purely economic dimension of the crisis. Man is precisely this: the spirit made flesh," he said.

The Pope's view is that it was a "spiritual" about-face that determined and accompanied the great social and ideological upheaval in Eastern Europe. But Mr. Gorbachev, in his article, ascribes to the Pope a concrete and determining influence over the course of events when he talks about his "great political role."

In what way, from the standpoint of the Vatican, can the actions of a Pope be "political"? "I do not believe that one can talk about a political role in the strict sense," replied the Pope, "because the Pope has as his mission to preach the Gospel. But in the Gospel there is man, and therefore human rights, freedom of conscience and everything that belongs to man. If this has a political significance, then, yes, it applies also to the Pope. But always speaking of man and defending man."

This liberation of man seemed beyond the horizon of his lifetime when the Pope arrived in Rome from Cracow for the conclave which would elect him Pope. "In 1978 when I became Pope, I did not think that I would be able to witness a transformation so radical as the one which has changed the face of Eastern Europe.

"Even in that great, unforgettable 1989—the year of the 'velvet revolution,' as the Czechoslovak President Havel defined it—there was just a sign, a glimmer, a trace of what would come later."

The Pope also spoke of last August's attempted coup against Mr. Gorbachev, marking the beginning of the end of the Soviet leader. "When the *coup d'etat* took place in the Soviet Union, I was in Hungary. We immediately released a statement of the Holy See in which we responded to the official news of Mr. Gorbachev's illness by wishing him a speedy recovery.

"The following day I recall the Mass celebrated in Heroes' Square in the center of Budapest. During the main ceremony I decided to add a passage to my homily, addressing what was happening in Moscow and worrying the entire world." The Pope remembered his prayer that day, "to ask God to spare that great nation from new tragedies and to invoke His aid in ensuring that the endeavors made in recent years to give back a voice and dignity to an entire society would not be placed in peril."

The Pope paid homage to Mr. Gorbachev for impelling the Soviet Union towards "the recognition of human rights and the dignity of man." While in the Vatican, Mr. Gorbachev had invited the Pope to Moscow.

"A lot has been said about the trip. Mikhail Gorbachev invited me and I believe that he sincerely hopes the visit will take place. And not just Gorbachev, but also his successor, even though one cannot strictly talk about a successor since Boris Yeltsin is president of Russia and not of the USSR.

"There is still work to be done on this trip before it can take place. No, it will not be in 1992. There is still work to be done," the Pope concluded. (Copyright 1992 by *Editrice La Stampa, S.p.A.*, Turin, Italy.)

5

THE FIRST
RUSSIAN PILGRIMAGE
TO FATIMA

The pilgrimage to Fatima of the Apostolic Administrator of the Republic of Russia, October 1991

On the seventy-fourth anniversary of the final apparition of the Mother of God, Fatima welcomed the first pilgrimage from Moscow. "With what emotion do we see today, in our midst, the first Apostolic Administrator for the Latin Catholics of the Republic of Russia, with his seat in Moscow, the Archbishop Dr. Tadeusz Kondrusiewicz," said Bishop emeritus Manuel de Almeida Trindade of Aveiro, who was presiding at the ceremonies in Fatima in October 1991. The gospel was intoned in Russian, and much of the Mass was sung in Latin and Greek as a symbol of unity. The Russians were greeted with enthusiastic applause by the crowds

Archbishop Tadeusz Kondrusiewicz

of pilgrims at Fatima, and it was the first time that Russians and Portuguese prayed together for the conversion of Russia.

At 45 years of age, Dr. Tadeusz Kondrusiewicz is one of the youngest bishops in the world. On October 20, 1989 he was consecrated in Rome by the Pope as Bishop of Minsk, the capital of Byelorussia, and a few months later the newly appointed bishop published a most informative article on the state of the Church in his country, in the May 1990 issue of *30 Days*. From that article we learn the interesting detail that, although Catholics were savagely persecuted and reduced in numbers by Communism, the faith has survived thanks to the family and the Rosary, which was substituted for Mass when there was no priest. Here is another moving testimony from Catholics of the Eastern bloc who were already living the message of Fatima long before it could reach them, and whose faith was preserved by Our Lady under the scourge of militant atheism. Today, despite facing enormous material problems, the Bishop said that their Church "is strong in faith, because the people of God have not deserted Christ, renewing themselves by family prayer, especially the Rosary." Rosary prayer groups have been organized, especially among young people, to visit and pray in churches for a month at a time. The Bishop was also preparing the celebrated icon of Our Lady of Ostra Brama in Vilnius to travel around from parish to parish.

On April 13, 1991, Bishop Kondrusiewicz was elevated by the Pope to the rank of Archbishop, and appointed to the post of Apostolic Administrator for the

Latin Catholics of the Republic of Russia, taking up his seat in Moscow for the first time since it had been vacated in 1936. His diocese covers nearly two million square miles and is served by just twenty priests. According to the Vatican, there are some 60,000 Catholics in Russia, of whom 10,000 are estimated to be in St. Petersburg. The Archbishop is being contacted by many groups of Catholic faithful, and has already registered with the authorities some forty new parishes.

On October 12th, the Archbishop celebrated his first Mass in Fatima at the Capelinha, and I am indebted to Fr. Francis Kerr, Chaplain to the Sacred Hearts Home for the Elderly at Clones in Ireland, for his kind permission to reproduce the report on the Archbishop's sermon which follows, as compiled from the detailed notes which he took during the sermon with the assistance of Sister Declan Mooney. Fr. Kerr was also in Fatima on pilgrimage, and concelebrated Mass with the Archbishop the next day, which he described as a deeply moving ceremony.

During his sermon, the Archbishop spoke of the Mother of God and referred to St. Bernard's saying, that never was it heard that Mary did not come to people's help when requested. He stated that in Portugal there was an image of Mary in every house, and in Russia there was the Icon of Our Lady of Kazan, which is similar to the image of Our Lady of Perpetual Help. When the Icon was taken into battle, the army never lost. In 1917 it was taken out of Russia and finally turned up at Sotheby's Auction Rooms in London, where it was said that an American purchased it for over £250,000. It eventually came to Fatima, where it was placed in the Byzantine Chapel, in the head-quarters of the World Apostolate of Fatima. While he was in Fatima, the Archbishop visited the chapel and prayed before the image, and on October 13 it was shown on the live television broadcast transmitted from Fatima to Moscow.

Archbishop Kondrusiewicz went on to say that as a human mother cares for her children, Mary would help them to know God and our heavenly fatherland. A human mother has special concern for the weakest of her children, and Russia is now the weakest child. He referred to the old Russian saying, "Without God, nothing is achieved." Russia is one of the richest countries, but in the last seventy years it has become one of the weakest in religion, and millions of people do not know God even exists.

He referred to the persecutions in the 1930s when many priests were sent to concentration camps or into exile. There was only one Catholic church in Moscow and one in Leningrad. After the Second World War, in the 1960s and 1970s, the persecution of the Church grew, and the Archbishop said he remembered the time when 16- and 17-year-old young people were not allowed to learn religion, in the hope that the Church would die. The Russian people retained the Rosary and hoped in the intercession of the Mother of God. In 1984, Pope John Paul II had consecrated the world and Russia to the Virgin Mary, and this was the conversion of Russia which they were now witnessing.

After the world was consecrated, there was a change in the Soviet Union and those in power had changed. A man who was considered to be an atheist had turned out to be "a weapon in the hand of God," and they had thrown off the shackles of Communism and were now united in the bonds of Christian love. Reforms were continuing in the Republic of Russia and the events in August showed that people would no longer be subjugated after tasting freedom. The victory of the Gospel and of democratic freedom were due to Mary and the Archangel Michael. Mary had broken the power of the evil serpent and Archangel Michael had won justice.

The Archbishop went on to say that a small group of Catholic and Orthodox pilgrims had come to the feet of Mary, to give thanks for the changes that had taken place. He added: "We commit the Church to her motherly care. We ask you, as at Cana, for new miracles—that Russia will turn to God. Yesterday when I arrived, I was told that the wood for the roof of the Chapel of Apparitions came from Russia." The Archbishop prayed that Russia would be covered with the roof of God's grace, that love would become dominant, and that there would be mutual respect among nations. He also appealed to his listeners for daily consecration to the Immaculate Heart of Mary.

On October 13th, over two hundred priests, including Archbishop Kondrusiewicz and twelve other bishops, took part in a concelebrated Mass, at which the principal celebrant, Bishop Manuel Trindade, delivered the following homily:

A well-known French historian summarized what happened in Russia exactly seventy-four years ago thus: "On the 6th of November (October 24 according to the Russian calendar) the insurrection broke out in the capital (at that time it was St. Petersburg, but the Soviets re-named it Leningrad); all the government buildings were occupied; on the 7th the revolution was victorious and the Soviets assumed power. The first Socialist State was born." (Jean Roux, in *Marxism Leninism*).

Now that almost three quarters of a century has passed, we can evaluate (or begin to evaluate) the costs of that revolution. The costs relating to the number of victims sacrificed were in the millions. There were costs also in liberties cut off and oppressions endured. In *The Gulag Archipelago*, Solzhenitsyn gives us a vivid portrayal of how human rights were trampled upon. There were still further costs because of the disproportion between the expenses involved and the results obtained. If Russia was for centuries a country where hunger was rampant, it can be seen today that abundance is no greater at the end of seventy-four years of collectivist experience. As a background for this bitter experience, it must be added that Russia was the first modern state in which atheism was imposed as an official ideology. It was there that Marx's expression became a classic one: "Religion is the opium of the people." If this is so—opium, that is, a dangerous and alienating drug—then it must be extirpated with the same determination with which society of today defends itself from narcotics and from those who cultivate them and engage in drug-dealing.

And there is no doubt that this was so. Russia—the Holy Russia of Orthodoxy—did not invent these expressions. They were imported from the West. Karl Marx—it is well not to forget this circumstance—was born in Trier, Germany. And all that Marx learned and later spread with the ardor of an apostle, was taught to him by philosophers and ideologists who dominated the culture of Central Europe.

And what was it that they taught? They taught that God does not exist, that there is no other reality beyond that which can be measured and touched, that human life ends with the dust in the tomb. And, about what refers to Jesus Christ, that such a man never existed; or if he existed, that we know little about him; that the miracles attributed to him, namely his Resurrection, are no more than legendary fables; that the Gospels which bear the names of Matthew, Mark, Luke and John were written in the middle of the second century and not by eye-witnesses. It was necessary to allow time for the legend to be composed. . . .

When we see these statements in books written by men of letters, we wonder about the acrobatics of the mind to which certain reasonings or fixed ideas are capable of subjecting the human intelligence. But these were the ideas which the October Revolution had imposed upon Holy Russia, whose history, molded by Christianity, was totally to the contrary. Now that the lid has been removed and the wall knocked down, it has come to light that the Christian faith remained hidden in the depth of the hearts of millions of people. Many of them paid with their lives, or with imprisonment or with exile for daring to say they were believers. Not all had the vocation to martyrdom: earning bread for their children often obliged them to guard in secret what they would have wished to proclaim to the four winds.

What underground currents will bind together the two extremes of Europe: this little Portugal, planted on the edge of the Atlantic Ocean, and that immense Russia, at the other end of Europe?

For seventy years now these underground currents have existed. It was not through the invention of reputable ideologies, but through the simple confession of three humble children, to whom the Virgin Mary appeared here and to whom she spoke. And she appeared precisely in the year and in the month (according to the Russian calendar) in which the revolution established the dictatorship of the proletariat and the atheism of the State of Russia. None of the children had heard the name of this country before, lost as they were on the heights of an arid rocky mountain region, watching their flocks, and belonging to families where letters were not a part of the daily bread that was eaten. But it was these children who transmitted the message heard from the lips of the Lady:

"Russia will spread her errors, but finally she will be converted." The fulfillment of this prophecy is now in sight. Religious liberty exists in Russia today. It is no longer necessary to conceal the faith in the refuge of one's conscience, as if it were a crime or a dark and repellent blot which has to be hidden from other eyes. People can now publicly profess their faith, whatever be their religious belief, without fear that the police will enter their home and carry them off to some gulag.

With what emotion do we see today, in our midst, the first Apostolic Administrator for the Latin Catholics of the Republic of Russia, with his seat in Moscow, the Archbishop Dr. Tadeusz Kondrusiewicz.

"Russia will be converted . . ." Conversion, however, is not a dress placed on a person from the outside. It is an attitude of the intelligence and of the heart. Conversion does not exist where there is no interior liberty—that liberty which consists not so much in the absence of fetters, as in the cult of truth, in self-control, in seeking rather to be than to appear to be, in seeking to be rather than to have. To be means cultivating the values that elevate man above the lower creatures, such as honesty of customs, sobriety of life, respect for the rights of others, invulnerability in the face of corruption, solidarity in regard to the needs of others.

In these points true Christian identity is by no means exhausted. To be a Christian means to believe that Jesus is the Word of God Incarnate, that He was crucified and died for us, and that after death He rose again and lives forever, that He is both the beginning and the end, the Alpha and the Omega, as the book of the Apocalypse says—of our collective history, as well as the history of this "unutterable" being who is in each one of us.

To be a Christian further signifies accepting the message—accepting and living by it—which Jesus Christ summed up in the eight Beatitudes, the first of which, "Blessed are the poor in spirit," is a resume of all the rest. The risk of societies in Eastern Europe is that, having escaped from the forms of slavery which were imposed on them from outside, they might now fall, of their own will, into other forms of slavery which are not lacking today in our hyper-civilized West: ambition for money, the cult of sex, the plague of consumerism.

What a misfortune it would be if what has happened in the East were merely a passing over from a collectivist economy to a market economy. Man is worth much more than that!

In Fatima, seventy-four years ago, the Virgin Mary made an appeal, through the three humble little shepherds, for conversion of the heart. May the Virgin Mary, who is the model for all believers and the icon and model of the Church—the Virgin Mary to whom all the Slavic peoples bear a filial and tender devotion—teach us, all of us, to be faithful as she was, to the end.

The Icon of Our Lady of Kazan

In his sermon, Archbishop Kondrusiewicz mentioned the Icon of Our Lady of Kazan, and how it came to be placed in the Byzantine chapel at Fatima. In view of its significance as a link between Russia and Fatima, I briefly recount the origins of the Icon and the development of its cult. The history of this sacred image is the subject of several differing points of view, and the following account is simply a resume of the version put forward by John Haffert on pages 312–314 of *Dear Bishop*, his book of memoirs concerning the history of the Blue Army.

The image came to light in the century when Russia began to emerge as a nation and the first czar was crowned, in 1547. Our Lady appeared to an eight-year-old girl and told her of a sacred image which had been hidden and lost during the time of the Mongolian and Mohammedan rule in the city of Kazan. After two further apparitions, the Icon was found in perfect preservation under the ruins of a burnt-out building, and taken to a church in Kazan whose pastor was Blessed Ermogen, later Patriarch of Moscow. He had an apparition of St. Sergei, one of the greatest saints in the history of Russia, who told him that this sacred image of Our Lady of Kazan would be the rallying point of the people and the means of saving and establishing the Russian nation.

Within a few years, this is indeed what happened. The kings of Sweden and Poland agreed to withdraw and peace was signed with Russia in 1613. From that time on the miraculous image of Our Lady of Kazan was known as "the Liberatrix and Protectress of Holy Mother Russia," and was invoked in all the crises of Russian history. It was taken to Moscow and enshrined in a cathedral opposite the Kremlin, but when Peter the Great decided to build a new capital to the north, at St. Petersburg, he ordered a magnificent new cathedral to be constructed, modeled after

St. Peter's Basilica in Rome, in which he intended to house the sacred Icon. This provoked an angry reaction from the citizens of Moscow, but it has not been satisfactorily established by historians whether the original remained in Moscow or was taken to St. Petersburg. Both cities possessed an icon, and both these icons became revered as sacred and holy images. Meanwhile, the copy of the Icon of Our Lady of Kazan in Kazan itself was stolen in 1904 and never recovered.

When the Communists took over Russia in November 1917, they turned the great Cathedral of Our Lady of Kazan in St. Petersburg into a museum of atheism. It then became the center of world militant atheism, and the Communist Party's official publications were produced on the printing presses which they installed in the crypt. Following the 1917 Revolution, the Communists seized all the Church's treasures and stored them in warehouses, and the use or possession of any article of religious significance was outlawed. In 1936 the Communists destroyed the former Cathedral of Our Lady of Kazan in Moscow, but according to John Haffert, when they subsequently tried to erect another building on the same site, to everyone's amazement there was such a continuous spate of accidents that finally men refused to work there. As a result, the Cathedral land was turned into a small green park.

Following the liberation of Russia from the yoke of militant atheism, that site, in the northwest corner of Moscow's famous Red Square, has now been returned to the Orthodox hierarchy. On page 12 of the

November/December 1991 issue of *Soul* magazine is a picture of the foundations of the original cathedral, which are being excavated at this moment, in preparation for the cathedral's reconstruction. The picture shows a wooden fence surrounding the site, and in the background the wall of the Kremlin and the building of the Council of Ministers, flying the red flag. The accompanying article by Peter Anderson, entitled "A time for hope in Russia," informs us that in November 1990, Patriarch Aleksy, the head of the Russian Orthodox Church, laid a special foundation stone for the cathedral in a ceremony which was attended by thousands, including the Russian President, Boris Yeltsin. The inscription on the stone states that the cathedral is "being rebuilt in memory of our Most Holy Queen, the Mother of God and ever Virgin Mary." Peter Anderson states that during the past three years, "amazing events and changes have occurred in this vast land. Russia is indeed being prepared for a great spiritual harvest."

As regards the sacred Icon of Kazan that is enshrined in the Byzantine Chapel of *Domus Pacis* in Fatima, it has not yet been definitively resolved how it made its way from Russia to the West, nor is it yet finally known whether this particular Icon of Our Lady of Kazan comes from Kazan, or from Moscow, or from St. Petersburg, or perhaps even from some other location. Those are matters which one hopes will in due course be clarified by historical research, but meanwhile there is no doubt about the genuine devotion which the Icon inspires, and, as the following story illustrates, this devotion is as relevant and efficacious today as ever, and may be found in some quite surprising places.

Until November 1990, Gennadi Gerasimov was the spokesman for the Soviet Foreign Ministry under President Gorbachev. Then he was appointed ambassador of the Soviet Union to Lisbon. On May 13, 1991 he went to Fatima and attended the Mass celebrated by Pope John Paul II. It was the first time that a Soviet ambassador had been present in the Cova da Iria during a religious ceremony. The interview with Gennadi Gerasimov which follows is taken from an article in the issue of October 18–24, 1991 of the Lisbon weekly, *Sabado*, entitled "Fatima—a triumph of the heart."

"Yes, it was the first time, but I had already been to Fatima twice before," Mr. Gerasimov told our reporter. "Before the 13th of May I had been to Fatima on a private visit with my wife and daughter." On that particular visit, the Soviet ambassador went to the Chapel of the Apparitions and the Byzantine Chapel, where he lit a candle. "Yes, it is true that I lit an enormous candle in the Byzantine Chapel at Fatima. I expect that it is still there," he added with a smile. Mr. Gerasimov was not very forthcoming on religious matters, but he told our reporter that he had been baptized. "We were all baptized in my house, myself, my wife and my daughter, aged twelve. We were all baptized and this never caused me any problems in the Party. It was a question that was never asked. They never asked if we were baptized or believed in God. . . ."

Today Gennadi Gerasimov once again has in his house an Icon of Kazan. "Yes, there is an Icon of Kazan in my house, and my wife has placed it on top of the table." A few years ago, it would not have been possible to imagine a Soviet ambassador talking in this way. Believer or not, Gerasimov is very interested to know all about Fatima and more especially the unique way in which Our Lady's apparitions relate to Russia. Before going to the Cova da Iria to be present at the Pope's Mass this May, the ambassador asked a Portuguese Catholic for a complete dossier on the apparitions and messages of Fatima.

Interview with José Correa, initiator of the Fatima-Moscow live TV transmission on October 13, 1991

The interview which follows has been translated from pages 13–17 of *Fatima-Moscou*, (Editions Tequi, Paris, November 1991), and is published here by kind permission of the author and publisher, Bertrand Lemaire. Mr. José Correa is Managing Director of the Catholic Radio and Television Network, based in Belgium, and he explains in this interview how the idea was conceived to make the live broadcast from Fatima to Moscow on October 13, 1991. It will be remembered that it was the Russian President, Boris Yeltsin, who authorized the transmission of this program to Moscow as a gesture of thanks for the loan of the radio station by Mr. Correa's organization, which Yeltsin had used to help defeat the August 1991 coup.

Mr. Correa, can you tell us how this idea came about, to make a live TV transmission between Fatima and Moscow?

"To be quite frank, the idea came from the Blessed Virgin . . . I was in Moscow on quite different business, and not for a second had this idea entered our heads. We were discussing the possibility of transmitting some video cassettes with the director of Russian TV, and I was explaining to him that in Brussels we make programs in the Russian language for the Soviet Union. This man then became very interested; he knew absolutely nothing about what the Catholic Church is or does, and what we think; his country had been totally isolated from Europe for decades, on account of the ideology of the regime, but from now on it is becoming possible to speak with them, and to show them what is happening elsewhere. He is an atheist, but like millions of Russians, he is immensely curious about everything that is happening in the West, including religion. For there really is a religious awakening in Russia, and most people, like him, are thirsty to find out and know about it.

"It was then that this director of Moscow Television asked me if I could offer him any suggestions for something which could be shown to the Soviet public illustrating religion in the West, the Catholic religion, perhaps a special event which would be of interest to the popular masses. I thought immediately of proposing Fatima: October 13 was not so far away, that feast always attracts a good many people, the ceremonies are very beautiful and touching, and at the same time, the transmission could be used for evangelization, by explaining the devotion to the Blessed Virgin, the role of prayer and penance, and of course the message of Fatima which is linked with Russia. The official accepted the suggestion immediately, and that was how the idea was conceived."

When you were planning this broadcast in Fatima and Moscow, did you prepare a list of the different questions that would be covered?

"Not at all, and that is where we were very much taken by surprise, for we were completely unaware what the reaction would be over there. Let me give you a summary of this live broadcast of seventy-five minutes between Fatima and Moscow, at 12:15 on October 13, 1991, with a repeat transmission to the non-Moslem republics of the Soviet Union in the evening. At the beginning, we had planned to set up a television platform with giant screens outside on Red Square in Moscow. Finally, on account of the cold at that time of the year, the Soviet organizers were led to transfer the platform and the screens into the great auditorium of the Novosti state news agency, where all the necessary equipment was readily available. There was a certain humorous aspect in all this, for it was in that very place that the Communist Party propaganda used to be conceived and disseminated!

"At Fatima, you will have seen that our platform was under the colonnades, on the right of the altar. First of all we showed a resume of the history of Fatima, lasting about ten minutes and covering the unfolding of the facts and the message; then we spoke of Sister Lucia, and we showed some shots of her Carmel at Coimbra; and then we showed the ceremonies live, such as the blessing of the sick, the Adeus or Farewell to the Virgin, and so on. In that way we gave the viewers some idea of the whole thing.

"Finally, we came to the moment when the presenter went over live to Moscow, and invited any person who would like to do so to ask a question. It was then that a young girl immediately asked the first question, which turned out to be the central question of the whole broadcast. The question was of union, and of unity between Christians. 'Why was there division between Christians?' She was insistent about it, it was very moving, I don't know if you heard it, but she said: 'You have devotion to the Blessed Virgin and we do too; you love her, and so do we; so why are we so separated? Why are there so many disputes?' This young girl was a Russian Orthodox.

"The program was carried by the Portuguese Catholic radio station, Radio Renascensa, (which had been inaugurated in the Sanctuary at Fatima on May 13, 1990 to transmit the Voice of Fatima more effectively—editor's note), and by the network of radio stations of the Russian federation. So more than three hundred radio stations carried the event, except for the Moslem republics. I believe that the Baltic States are considering transmitting the program in their own languages. . . .

"I believe that in the light of our experience, this is just a beginning. The Soviet TV producer who is here is quite delighted; he says that it is a first step, and that we must get to know each other better. A certain official in Moscow said a lovely thing: 'We need to know each other in order to like each other, so we must get to know each other more.'"

In the course of the broadcast, was the sense of the division between Catholics and Orthodox noticeable?

"Yes, as I said, all the questions from Moscow centered on the division, all the questions! The Catholics.who were here on the platform at Fatima had not at all imagined that the program would be centered on this question, but rather on devotion to the Blessed Virgin, the message of Fatima, and the question of the religious situation in the USSR today, but all the questions from Moscow revolved around this subject."

At the end of the interview, José Correa mentioned the moving message addressed to the Russian people by Fr. Werenfried van Straaten at the end of the program. The text of this address is reproduced in full in the next section, but before going on to that, there are one or two other interesting items about the program which should be included in this account.

During the course of the transmission, a long explanation was given on the value that the solemn benediction at the end of the Mass would constitute to each person who would receive it in truth, no matter where they were or how remote their location might be in Russia. Bertrand Lemaire mentions another interesting detail, namely that this special program of seventy-five minutes from Fatima made such an impact on the Russian people that the film was televised again on November 7. Was it simply a coincidence that November 7 was the anniversary of the Communist Revolution?

Further information about the live television broadcast from Fatima to Moscow was published in the September/December 1991 bulletin of *The Seers of Fatima*, from which the following details have been taken, with the kind permission of the editor, Fr. Louis Kondor, SVD. For the transmission, the Sanctuary was also connected with Polish radio and television, as well as with various other European radio and television stations, and with 380 cable television services from the United States. The Bishop of Leiria-Fatima addressed a brief message to the Russian people, and at the beginning of the program, one of the Soviet journalists exclaimed, "just two years ago we would have been hanged for making this transmission!" One Russian housewife also touchingly commented, "the most important thing to know was that there were many people thinking of us and praying for us."

The report in *The Seers of Fatima* concluded with the very encouraging information that the book, *Fatima in Lucia's Own Words* has just been published in the Russian language, and that part of this edition will go directly to Russia to be distributed *gratis*, through the ecclesiastical bodies now functioning there.

A message from Fatima to our brothers in Russia

At the conclusion of the Fatima-Moscow television broadcast, Fr. Werenfried van Straaten, the famous founder of the organization, *Aid to the Church in Need*, delivered the following message to the peoples of Russia, which is reproduced here with Fr. van Straaten's kind permission from the December 1, 1991 issue of his newsletter, *Mirror*. In the same issue Fr. van Straaten stated that the broadcast was carried by 150 television stations, reaching an estimated audience of between thirty and forty million people.

You are children of Mary, a mother who never abandons her little ones. That is why she, whom you venerate as Our Lady of Kazan and Patroness of Russia, turned her maternal gaze to your country when, in 1917, she took up the struggle against Lenin's revolution that was a total uprising against God.

Before anyone knew that Lenin was already on his way to Russia to unleash the revolution, six times Mary called Western Christendom to prayer, conversion, penance and consecration to her Immaculate Heart, so that Russia would be converted instead of becoming Satan's henchman and the ruin of countless souls. For Mary added to her appeal, "If my requests are heeded, Russia will be converted; if not it will spread its errors throughout the whole world, unleashing wars and religious persecutions. Many good people will be martyred, the Holy Father will have much to suffer and entire peoples will be destroyed." God confirmed these words with the miracle of the sun.

The miracle of Fatima did not convince the world. Will the miracles which God has performed over the past two years in your country convince the unfaithful West? For the West has not been converted. That is why Communism is not dead. It is in hiding. It is waiting for its hour to come. The hour of the putsch in Moscow. Or the hour to attack in Croatia. Where will it strike tomorrow? In East and West many people live in fear. . . .

Faced with this dramatic situation, we must do everything we can to meet the demands these times confront us with. For we cannot think that God who is checking the advance of Communism, has nothing to say to Western Christianity which in so many ways denies the teachings of Christ, and scandalizes you who have forsworn belief in Marx and are now seeking God.

We shall pray that the Lord may help you to resolve your problems and grant you happiness and peace. For your part, you must pray that God may purify us, so that our inconsistent Christianity may not hinder union with you who have been refined by suffering. For it is not without reason that in Fatima Mary said that our conversion must precede that of Russia.

And let us all become like children who cry out in mortal fear to their mother. Let us turn to Mary and pray the Rosary for the conversion of Russia and of the materialistic West. Pray as the ancients prayed: like Moses on the mountain and Jonah in the belly of the whale. Like the young men in the furnace and like Job when he was tested by Satan.

The prayers of all of them were heard. Let us pray with unshakable trust and with a heart which embraces the whole world in love. And the Lord will incline His ear to us and His mercy will know no bounds.

6

THE TESTIMONY
OF
BISHOP HNILICA

Bishop Hnilica and the Message of Fatima

Archbishop Kondrusiewicz was accompanied on his visit to Fatima by Bishop Pavol Hnilica, SJ, the Slovak Bishop who has worked for a long time to spread the message of Fatima, particularly with regard to Russia. It will be remembered that it was Bishop Hnilica who had taken all the Fatima documentation to John Paul II during his convalescence in 1981, and who had presented him with the statue of the Immaculate Heart of Mary which the Holy Father sent to a specially constructed church on the Polish-Soviet border. It was during the time he spent in prison in Czechoslovakia that Bishop Hnilica discovered the true meaning of Our Lady's request to consecrate Russia to her Immaculate Heart as the only way to obtain peace in the world. As a result, he has worked to spread the message of Fatima wherever he went. The following account of Hnilica's work is taken from the interview with the Bishop's secretary, printed on pages 28–31 of Bertrand Lemaire's recent study, *Fatima-Moscou* (Editions Tequi, Paris, November 1991). It is published here by the kind permission of the author.

Hnilica was consecrated Bishop in Czechoslovakia at the age of thirty by his own bishop, who was near death. Owing to the persecution, his consecration could not be carried out in an official manner, and his bishop gave him a special mission, to help the Church in the East: "Your diocese stretches from Berlin to Moscow and Peking." Hnilica took this mission very seriously, and for forty years he brought help to many bishops and evangelized many people at the risk of his life. He came to Rome, where he founded a religious association called *Pro Deo et Fratribus* (for God and the brethren), and his work consisted in supporting people spiritually, with Bibles and Gospels, and also materially, with money.

It was not until long afterwards that his episcopal consecration was officially recognized by Pope Paul VI. They met at Fatima in 1967, and spoke with Lucia. Bishop Hnilica knows her very well, and has spoken with her several times about Russia. So he has been known as a bishop since the pontificate of Paul VI, and thus he was able to work in a manner which was more or less unofficial but very effective.

... Last week, Bishop Hnilica came to Fatima to celebrate this marvel of the Lord, and to speak

Bishop Pavol Hnilica, SJ

with the Archbishop of Moscow about this evangelization of Russia.

Bishop Hnilica now declares without ceasing that the triumph announced by the Blessed Virgin at Fatima will only be possible if the Catholic and Orthodox Churches are reconciled. In his view, it is there that the profound meaning of the message is to be found. The promise "in the end my Immaculate Heart will triumph" will only be possible if the two churches become one, and Bishop Hnilica says that this work of ecumenism should be lived and brought about in the dimension of charity; dialogue can only bear fruit in charity. At this moment, Russia needs help to rebuild the Church, for everything was destroyed by Communism. The other brothers and sisters of the Catholic Church can make contact with their Orthodox brothers and sisters in the dimension of charity, which is the most authentic sign of true Christianity. . . .

A few months ago, on his last trip to Russia, Bishop Hnilica was able to speak with representatives of the Orthodox Church and to suggest this fraternal collaboration to help the Russian people to eat, and to obtain spiritual as well as material nourishment. The person whom he met said to him: "We beg you, help us, because otherwise we will not succeed." For this reason, he speaks about this reconciliation, for the triumph of a Mother is only possible if the daughter and the son are reconciled. In order to triumph, the Immaculate Heart of Mary needs our hearts, and *heart* means, in the first place, fraternal charity."

Bishop Hnilica's Homily at Marienfried

Several years ago, in 1988, Bishop Hnilica was invited to speak to the Marian Federation at Marienfried, near Ulm in Germany. During the Mass on July 24, he gave a most interesting homily in which he recounted some of the unique experiences that befell him as he sought to become, first a seminarian and then a priest behind the former Iron Curtain. His homily, which was subsequently published as a pamphlet entitled: *ROME—MOSCOW—FATIMA: The Consecration of Russia to the Mother of God,* brings out a number of important topics that are central to my study, and I am most grateful to Bishop Hnilica for his permission to include it here. The text is reproduced as translated from the German, with only one or two slight omissions from the original:

Praise be to Jesus Christ! My dear brothers and sisters!

I am here at Marienfried for the first time. Marienfried is a surprise to me! When I first came, I looked around, and what did I find to my joy? The sign of Mary of the Latter Times! The sign of the latter times is at the same time the sign of the first times. The first account of Mary—or the first sign of Mary—can be found in the so-called Proto-evangelium. There it says, "I will put enmity between you and the woman, between your seed and her seed. And she will crush your head." What does this account tell us? It speaks of a victory. But also the last account, the one of the latter times, talks about a victor: a woman clothed with the sun. It all started in Lourdes. In Lourdes the Mother of God introduced herself as the Immaculate Conception. Pope Pius IX took the theological and biblical proof for the Immaculate Conception from the Proto-evangelium: "I will put enmity between you and the woman, and she will crush your head" (Gen 3:15). Mary appeared in Lourdes and identified herself: "I am the victor of all times." Just at the time when the serpent raised its head through atheistic Marxism, Mary spoke in Fatima: "I am the victor." May I recall some of these victories to your mind?

There was the sea battle of Lepanto, for instance, when Europe was threatened by the Turks. The Turkish fleet was far superior to the Christian fleet. What did Pope Pius V do? He mobilized all the Christian kings and their soldiers and called all of Christendom to pray the Rosary. The then Sultan, Suleiman the Magnificent, was reported to have said, "I am not afraid of the Christian kings, of their cannons and fleets and generals, but I am afraid of their prayer." That prayer is the Rosary.

We all know how this sea battle ended. During the Pope's prayer in Rome, he had a vision where he saw how both opposing fleets clashed. At this moment he also saw how the Mother of God spread her mantle over the Christian soldiers. They won. In Venice there is still today a painting of this battle with the inscription, "Not through our power, nor through our cannons, nor through our courage, but through your help have we won."

The same happened when the Turks stood before Vienna in 1683 with an army 200,000 strong. Jan Sobieski advanced from Tsehenstochau with his 30,000 soldiers praying the Rosary. They had all received a medal from the Cardinal of Tarnawa.

Imprinted on one side there was a picture of the Sorrowful Mother of God; on the other the word "Mary." When they attacked the Turks on September 12, they shouted, "Jesus, Mary, help! Help us! Be at our side!" And they won. We could give so many examples. But the Mother of God had prophesied her greatest victory at Fatima: "In the end my Immaculate Heart will triumph." This means that Love will triumph—the truth, the good, the mercy of God. The Heart of Mary is a song of the mercy of the heavenly Father. This mercy will triumph, but with one condition: the conversion of Russia. This is what I will mainly speak about. "Russia will be converted." This statement comes from Pope Pius XII. The message of Fatima is one of the greatest interventions of God through Mary in world history since the death of the apostles. Only in the name of God does the Mother of God intervene. She doesn't say a word, doesn't take a step, without the explicit will of God. Pope Pius XII further says: "You cannot understand this message if you don't know atheistic Communism, if you don't know what happened in Russia." I want to add some statements of the popes about this battle with atheistic Communism.

Pope Pius XI says about this militant atheism: "Today we see something that world history has never seen before: The waving of the flag of Satan in the battle against God and religion, against all peoples, and in all parts of the world; a phenomenon that outdoes all that happened before. Atheistic Communism surpasses all previous persecutions in the Church, even that of Nero or Diocletian, not only in its extent, but also in its violence. The whole world is threatened with falling back into a barbaric state, a state worse than before Christ came." These are weighty words. The world in the time before Christ was not against God. It had lost friendship with God, but it was searching for God. Today for the first time a part of humanity is against God. For the first time in history we see a cold-bloodedly planned and very precisely prepared battle that has turned against religion and against everything that is Godly. In this battle everything really revolves around the central question of the most important decision in this world: will man be for or against God. This decision determines human destiny. Could the one who was commissioned by God from all eternity remain indifferent? The hour of the battle against God is the hour of Mary, not only in this Marian year, but in this whole period of time. The Marian year will come to an end, but it was the intention of the Holy Father to start a Marian epoch with this year.

Pope John XXIII said, "The prince of this world (Lucifer) has always been in battle against God. But what we see today is a battle that has flared up throughout the whole world." He was referring to atheistic Communism. I can quote for you what the atheists say. For instance, Lenin declares, "God is my personal enemy. I prefer an atheistic exploiter or a billionaire to a believing proletarian." About ten years ago thc Communist newspaper, *The Moscow Evening News*, wrote: "We don't fight against the believers, nor do we fight against priests. We fight against God, to wrench the believers from him." In the place of God they put the Party. Listen to what they (the Russian Communists) say about Lenin, "Lenin: a name of unending greatness. He is like a star that sends its light against the centuries. Lenin's flag goes higher and higher. Lenin is as immortal as life itself." And about the Party: "The Party, the Party, the Party gave us everything, sun and wind! Never was she greedy; wherever she was, there was life. And what we are, we are through her, through the Party." This is the greatest blasphemy that was ever pronounced by a human being in all of history. This is something satanic. Could Mary remain indifferent? And the children of Mary, can we remain indifferent in facing this challenge? She has surpassed all challenges. Satan challenged God directly through the Russian Revolution in 1917. And to this challenge Mary answered in Fatima in 1917, "In the end my Immaculate Heart will triumph." Love and mercy will triumph, not hatred. But only with us and through us. Mary does everything that is necessary. But we also must not remain inactive.

This, I think, holds true also for you here in Marien-fried. Here the Mother of God appears as the "Mediatrix omnium gratiarum," as the mediatrix, as the victor.

One can only mediate after a victory. We have to contribute to this victory of love and mercy.

Now I want to tell you how this victory is already unfolding. Can we actually win? Certainly! We are one hundred percent sure that we will win because the Mother of God said so in the name of God. God wants it! We fight a fight that is already determined. God cannot lose; therefore the Mother of God cannot lose. We are already the victors. If the soldiers know that their generals are convinced of the victory, they will go into battle with great joy and enthusiasm. We have this guarantee: we are the victors. We lose only when we dissociate ourselves from God, from Christ. But the Apostle Paul asks, "Who can separate us from the love of Christ?" All of hell can't, all of humanity can't—nobody! Only I, myself, can make that decision.

Now about my personal story. As you know, I come from Czechoslovakia, a country where we have experienced this battle. When the persecution by the atheistic Communists began, all the bishops were arrested first, then the seminaries were closed and the seminarians were brought to various work camps. After that, thousands of the best religious priests, nuns, and brothers were arrested; then the diocesan priests, and finally, the rest of the religious priests and brothers. In the space of one night they were all brought to various concentration and work camps: Jesuits, Salesians, Franciscans, etc. Later, 10,700 nuns of all the religious orders were taken. Today they are still in these camps, those that are still living. Tens of thousands of lay people were imprisoned, all the books were confiscated and destroyed, so that the state secretary of culture could say very proudly, "The Church is amputated at the knee." The poor secretary didn't know that the Church, when wounded at the knee, is by no means totally destroyed. She is still powerful and she will remain powerful.

A bishop in prison once said: "The Communists took into account all the human strategies to destroy the Church. They imprisoned the bishops, the priests, the religious, and those in the lay apostolates. But they forgot the main element: the Holy Spirit. They will lose this battle, and they are already in the process of losing it." At this moment, in Russia, in Poland, and in Czechoslovakia we find that there is a religious enthusiasm awakening that has never been seen before. A short time ago there was a Marian pilgrimage to the shrine in Lewotscha. About 300,000 pilgrims took part in it. Most of them came on foot because the trains and buses were on strike. What enthusiasm! And that bishop continued, "I'm sure that our people will be faithful to our dear God and to the Catholic Church, because they revere the heart of Mary and the heart of Jesus so much." When the persecutions started, something else started too: devotion to Mary. We all looked to the protection of Mary. For example, we copied thousands—tens of thousands—of the little booklet of Louis-Marie Grignion de Montfort, *True Devotion to Mary*, with a hand press, because we didn't have any more religious printing shops. Bibles were copied in the same way.

May I tell you briefly about my own experiences? At that time I was neither a priest nor a bishop. I was a seminarian. At midnight we were awakened. Three policemen forced their way into our rooms. There were three of us in the room. "Get up! Follow us!" Outside there were three buses waiting and everybody had to sit down beside his "guardian angel," as we called the policemen. They were armed with machine guns. We drove into the unknown. What happened inside of me? I was afraid. I was almost desperate. I wasn't afraid of heavy work, which was the most likely fate that would await us in a work camp. In the past I had been a manual laborer for six years and I was used to heavy work. I was afraid that I could never be a priest.

The priesthood was the only yearning I had in my life, my only longing, my future, my joy, my happiness. And this I owe to my mother's prayers. She prayed for this when she was still a girl and not yet married. I was the first of eight children. Together with the Mother of God, she brought her sacrifices to God and with it this petition. But none of us was able to study. We were poor. But she continued to pray. She continued to pray and to do her work around the house. Then I started studying and entered the novitiate with the Jesuits. There was war. The bombs fell. Often we would cower in the cellar. Often our superior gave us absolution— maybe twenty or thirty times—during the days of greatest danger. During these moments I didn't pray. I struggled with our dear Lord, "Let me live, let me live! Allow me, at least once, to offer a single Holy Mass! Then I will be ready to die."

But when we sat in the buses and drove to the unknown, maybe to Siberia, I thought, "That's it. You can never become a priest!" Again dark clouds overshadowed my soul. Again my heart started to cry out, "Lord, allow me to offer at least one Holy Mass. Allow me to become a priest!" To get relief from these dark clouds, I took the Sacred Scriptures and opened them up. And what did I read? These were the words, "Did not the Messiah have to undergo all this, so as to enter into His glory?" I was shaken. This was the most striking answer from Heaven for my present situation. Before that I was desperate. Now a quiet entered into my heart that I had never known before. Suddenly, I realized that the essence of the priesthood is the Cross, suffering, and sacrifice. And the light of this Cross shone on all of us in the camp.

There were seven hundred seminarians and religious in our camp. I won't tell you about the external circumstances. But there was something we felt very deeply, that which we heard in today's gospel, "Woman, behold your son! Behold your mother!"

We said to the Mother of God, "You are our mother now. Your Son gave you to us on Calvary, and we are on Calvary now. You must not leave us!" Never did we have so much childlike trust and never did we experience so much help.

One day my parents came to the camp. I was there together with one of my younger brothers. We were not allowed to speak. One day we were working outside by the river. There was a dirt road near where we were. When my mother came by, together with some other people, the policemen thought they were farmers from the town and didn't hinder them. When they came closer and passed by, my mother only said, "My children, be faithful to our dear Lord and to your vocation, even if you have to die for them!" That's the right response of a mother. Never have I understood the sorrowful Mother of God so well as in that hour. She offered up her divine Son to the heavenly Father for us, for the salvation of the world.

I was ordained a priest in a hospital, in a room of the quarantine unit. At that time all the bishops of our country had been arrested. There was no one free who could ordain me. One of them was an outpatient in this hospital. But he was constantly accompanied by three "guardian angels," three policemen. The doctor who treated him was a Christian. On the day of my ordination, he told the security guards, "Today the patient has to be treated in the unit for contagious diseases." The policemen were afraid of being infected and let the bishop go into the unit by himself. I was there already. And so I was ordained a priest. It's very hard to describe what I felt. I felt the mercy, the love, the kindness, but also the power of God. I had given up hope of becoming a priest. But now I realized that for God nothing is impossible. What made a great impression on me was the fact that it was the feast day of the Archangel Michael, September 29. One hour before the arrival of the bishop I still didn't know if my ordination would take place. I told St. Michael, "You have selected this day for me." And I took his name, Michael, which means "Who is like God?" Whenever I was in danger, I said to myself, "Why be afraid? The police force of the Communists can be hundreds of thousands times stronger; against God it is nothing and will remain nothing."

On that day I said to our dear Lady, "Now you are my only mother." I consecrated myself to her in a special way. I could not meet my natural mother, who had prayed for me so much. Therefore, she did not know anything about my ordination to the priesthood. I was ordained a bishop three months later in a basement. I fought against it. But my provincial ordered me to accept this ordination under obedience, so I agreed. It is not popular any more to obey, but thirty-seven years ago it was different. I was afraid of this great responsibility. On the way, on the train, I prayed, "Dear God, let this train be derailed so that I will not get there alive." This fear disappeared suddenly when, in the basement, the bishop started Holy Mass with these words, "In the name of Jesus every knee shall bow, in heaven, on earth and also in hell." Even Satan has to bow his knee. It struck me like lightning: "Why are you afraid? Not you, but Christ is the victor. He has won already. You have only to remain a humble instrument in His hand." This gave me the strength to let everything pass over me.

Finally, I would like to point out two things. Every bishop has to swear several oaths. First, to spread the Gospel, for Christ has commanded: "Go forth to the whole world and bring my message to every creature." This he said to his Apostles, and the bishops are the successors of the Apostles. Second, fidelity to the pope, fidelity to the Holy Father. This my mother had taught me long ago. Every day we prayed for the Holy Father, and I continued this even later, when I became a Jesuit. The Jesuits used to be uniquely proud of being subject to and obedient to the Holy Father in a special way. I prayed for him even more in the concentration camp. The reason for our being arrested was for fidelity to the Holy Father in Rome. In the camp a political commissar told us, "You can be free immediately, you can go home, but under this condition: you have to acknowledge the Patriarch of Moscow instead of the Pope in Rome." This opened our eyes. Satan knows what the foundation of the Church is: It is Peter. Only to him was it promised, ". . . the gates of Hell will not prevail against it." Hell wants to destroy this foundation. The victory over Satan is promised only to the Church that is in union with Peter. And later Christ said, "Peter, Satan has desired to have you that he might sift you like wheat. But I have prayed for you that your faith may not fail."

At that time in the basement I swore fidelity to Peter with all my heart. You know that every bishop receives a diocese when he is ordained. I was told, "Your diocese covers Peking–Moscow–Berlin." This was not meant geographically but symbolically. I didn't understand it at the time. Thirty years later, when I was allowed to concelebrate Mass with the Holy Father, I said to him afterwards at breakfast, "Holy Father, only you have a bigger diocese. It comprises the whole world. Mine comes right after that in size: Peking–Moscow–Berlin." The Pope said, "Paul, this is your mission field. Find yourself the best Christians as missionaries!"

Surely you have heard about the attempt on the life of the Pope in St. Peter's Square in Rome on May 13th, 1981. This attempt has brought us closer to the message of Fatima, and it made the message more clearly felt, because this attempt was already predicted. Even the Holy Father admitted that. As head of the Church, he is the one primarily concerned, but the message referred to all of us. During his time in the hospital, he wanted to know all about Fatima. I gave him all the available documents. After his release from the hospital, I brought him a statue of Our Lady of Fatima which some

German pilgrims, who had been in Rome during the assassination attempt, had brought from Fatima. They wanted to give it to the Holy Father as a present. For three months it was in my chapel. It was the most beautiful statue I had ever seen. It was hard for me to part with it when I presented it to the Holy Father. And what did he say to me? "Paul, in these three months I have come to understand that the only solution to all the problems of the world, the deliverance from war, the deliverance from atheism, and from the defection from God, is the conversion of Russia. The conversion of Russia is the content and meaning of the message of Fatima. Not until then will the triumph of Mary come." The Holy Father had a chapel built on a hill on the eastern frontier of Poland—on the frontier of Russia—and put the statue there. The Mother of God looks toward Russia. But she wants us to look toward Russia as well.

When I accompanied the Holy Father as he was returning from Fatima, he asked me, "Paul, when and how will we be successful in converting Russia?" The conversion of Russia is a strong desire of the Holy Father's heart, because he knows the third mystery of Fatima, and the desire of Mary. He wants *Totus tuus*, to belong to Mary totally. I answered him, "Padre Pio is reported to have said, 'Russia will be converted, if you find as many Christians as there are atheists.' And that is the message of Fatima: believe, pray, adore and love God for all those who don't, and for those who most need the mercy of God."

I don't have to explain to you the message of Fatima. Then I said to the Holy Father, "Perhaps we can be more optimistic than Padre Pio. What do we read in the Old Testament? Thousands and tens of thousands of the inhabitants of the towns of Sodom and Gomorrah would have been saved, if ten just men had been found." And the Holy Father made a gesture with his hands and asked, "How many just men are necessary today to save the world?" A very serious question, spoken by the highest authority in all of Christendom, the vicar of Christ. And we can answer as in those days. God entrusted salvation to Abraham. If he had found the ten just men and if he had had more trust to ask for salvation for the sake of five just men, the towns would have been saved.

Today our Lady has this mission. She is not lacking in trust. But she has to find a certain number. Today she is looking for those souls, those "ten just men." That means the number of the just who are necessary today. I am convinced Marienfried is a sign of this. Mary is looking for the necessary victim souls, those children who are praying for others. Because that is the message of Marienfried, to pray for sinners. I have often met with Sister Lucia of Fatima. Once she said to me, "Father, the first request of the Mother of God to us was to be ready to accept the daily crosses which God will send to us, and to offer them for sinners. In later requests, she asked that we offer them especially for Russia. When she mentioned this country for the first time, *Russia*, we children thought that this meant a certain woman, perhaps a sinner, for whom we should pray." And indeed, it is a great woman, a big country, on whose behalf the Mother of God steps in. After all, she is committed to God.

And we? Haven't we neglected her? For seventy years we have not taken the essential message of Fatima seriously enough, namely the conversion of Russia.

The present bishop of Fatima once told me, "I was the secretary to the former bishop. He interviewed Lucia, and built the sanctuary of Fatima. At the end of his life he was paralyzed. As his secretary I was also his driver. One time as he limped toward me on his cane and said, 'Let us bring Mary to Moscow, to Russia!' I had to laugh. How could we bring the statue of Mary to Russia? Should I drive the car there? A paralyzed bishop with a statue in his hands all the way to Russia?"

But today, twenty years later, after the time I spent in the concentration camp in Czechoslovakia, during which we studied the message of Fatima, I understand what the bishop meant in those days: "The message of Fatima applies to Russia. Fatima and Russia are one."

You, here in Marienfried, are venerators of Fatima. The meaning of your life is the apostolate of Fatima. We have to bring Mary to Russia. Only then will the triumph of Mary come.

As you know, the Holy Father consecrated Russia to the Immaculate Heart of Mary on March 25, 1984, in the year of the Redemption. He invited all bishops to do the same, each in his own diocese.

But my diocese, symbolically, is Moscow. For thirty years, therefore, I had been trying to go to Moscow, but always in vain.

But then, on the day of the consecration of Russia, I was in Moscow, and I performed the consecration in Moscow, in spiritual union with the Holy Father! How could this happen? I worked with Mother Teresa in Calcutta. In February 1984, I was with her in Calcutta. Because the Soviet officials there didn't know me, I applied for a visa to Moscow for March 22 to 25, and I received it! Mother Teresa asked all her sisters to pray. Those sisters said a novena for the consecration. Accompanied by a priest, whom I ordained for Russia at Fatima just a few months before, I arrived at the airport in Moscow at four o'clock in the morning. The controlling inspector asked me for my passport, and inquired if I was the person in the photograph. I had an Italian passport and I answered in Italian. The inspector didn't understand me, but I realized I had to pretend to be an Italian. Then he began to telephone. Outside it was ten degrees below zero. But it wasn't cold for me, I was sweating, perhaps more than I am now under the sun. The priest beside me was sweating too. Jokingly, he had said to me in Calcutta, "Father Paul, we are going to Moscow for four or five days, but perhaps it will turn into fourteen years in Siberia." It seemed that he might be right. I took out my Rosary, which Mother Teresa had given me, and I began to pray. The inspector was inside still phoning. But, thanks be to God, no

one answered. It was four o'clock in the morning.
The people that he tried to call slept well. The inspector didn't give up. He came out and asked me
some questions. I answered again, "Si, si." He disappeared and phoned again. For a very long time. I
had prayed nearly the whole Rosary and I said to
the Mother of God, "I am totally in your hands.
May the will of the Lord be done." When the official
still didn't get any answer, he became very angry.
He hung up, stamped my passport and said, "Beat
it!" But after that came the baggage check. They
searched the bag in which I had my episcopal cross,
Bible, and different medals. I had hundreds of miraculous medals of the Mother of God and a few
medals of the Vatican with me, perhaps sixty. The
soldier took them in his hand and I could see that he
liked them. He asked me: "What are these?" I told
him, "Souvenirs from Rome." And I said, "Comrade, if you like them, you may take some." And he
took some. I can testify that the Rosary and the
medals opened the gates of Moscow for me.

The high point of my stay in Moscow was the
feast of the Annunciation of Our Lady. It was a Saturday, and the Kremlin was open to tourists. So I
planned it. I was a tourist too. But already at the en-
trance I had difficulties. I was supposed to hand
over my bag with the "certain things" in it for safe-
keeping. The guard said, "That must remain here."
That I didn't like at all. So I begin to chat with him:
where does he come from, does he have children,
what are their names? "Konstantinus and Michael."

I congratulated him: "You have selected beautiful names." (They are Christian names.) "Where are your children staying?" "With Babushka (Grandmother)."There they are in good hands." (The grandmothers in Russia are mostly still believers.) He became more and more friendly. At last I said to him, "You know, comrade, I need this bag. Inside there are personal things. And he said, "All right, an exception. Go!" So I entered the first church. In the Kremlin all the churches had been changed into museums. I asked the attendant: "What church is this?" "The church of Saint Michael!" she answered with enthusiasm. "A church of Saint Michael, how great," I answered, and then I asked, "Do you know who Michael is?" "Yes, he is an archangel." This she said with great enthusiasm. I asked further, "Are you a believer?" She answered bravely, "Yes, I'm a believing woman." And I said, "I too am a believer." But I didn't say who I was. To confess her faith look a lot of courage.

The name Michael means "Who is like God?" Who is as great as God, as good as God? Today a struggle against God has broken out in the whole world, not only in Russia, but also in the West, where I come from. But for us as Christians it is the sign of victory. Nobody is like God. We will triumph. And I said, "My name is Michael too." (I took it at my ordination.) And she said, "Then this is also your church. Welcome." Can you see you how our dear Lord sometimes jokes? So I entered my church. I went to the altar of St. Michael, I took out the Communist newspaper *Pravda* from my bag and I spread it out. However, between the pages of *Pravda* was *L'Osservatore Romano* with the text of the Pope's consecration of Russia. And I began to pray, "We have recourse to your protection . . ." and "we are imploring you, O Holy Mother of God . . ." I think those are the most beautiful Marian prayers. You should pray them often! There, in a church of the Kremlin, I united myself with the Holy Father and with all the bishops of the world; and so, in union with them, I consecrated Russia to the Immaculate Heart of Mary.

After that I went to the Marian church of the Assumption of Our Lady. Here I repeated the consecration at the altar of the Mother of God. On the opposite side there is the throne of the Patriarch. I put a medal on top of it and I said to our Lady, "As soon as possible you have to bring the true patriarch to this throne." Again I took out the Communist newspaper with *L'Osservatore Romano* inside, united myself spiritually with the Holy Father and with all the other bishops, and said the prayers again attentively. I said Holy Mass in this church too! How could I do that? Well, I pretended to take a photo. An empty bottle of aspirin tablets was my chalice. I arranged wine and a few drops of water so that they were handy. The hosts were in a little nylon bag. That's all that is necessary for a Holy Mass: bread and wine. The Latin text of the Mass for the feast of the Annunciation of Mary was in the pages of *Pravda*. *Pravda* means truth. Maybe that was the first time the whole truth was in that newspaper—the text of the Annunciation of the Lord to Mary.

That was the most moving Holy Mass of my entire life. It left me shaken. I felt the great power of God, God's love, God's kindness. Communism to me seemed so small; all dangers were so little, they didn't exist any more. Only God and Mary. At the Offertory I renewed the consecration of Russia to Mary. I said one part of the consecration prayer right after the Consecration of the bread and wine, when the living Savior was present. It was the part where it is written: "In a special way we entrust and consecrate to you those individuals and nations which particularly need to be thus entrusted and consecrated," (namely the nations of Russia).

When I told all this to the Holy Father, he was convinced that it was a sign for him. He had great difficulties getting even some of the bishops and cardinals in Rome to perform that consecration. Once I spoke with Cardinal Ratzinger for two hours on a plane. As you know, he is the right hand man of the Holy Father. When I told him all of this, he also said that it was not easy to get this consecration through. As I said, it was a sign for the Holy Father. God wants this consecration. For He even sent a Catholic bishop to Moscow on that date in order to perform the consecration there, together with all the bishops of the world. The Holy Father said to that bishop, "On that day, Paul, the Mother of God led you by the hand." "No, Holy Father," I answered, "she carried me in her hands, in her arms."

I'm sure I said the prayer "We have recourse to your protection" and "Under your shield" at least one hundred times in the streets of Moscow, on the trains and on the buses. Every Christian should say these prayers every day for the conversion of atheists, but also for himself, and he should offer his own crosses and problems as gifts to God. This is the victory of Mary. She wants to activate all her children for this victory, for the conversion of Russia. Not the destruction of Russia, but its conversion. Again and again I stood in Red Square, in front of the tomb of Lenin, where soldiers keep an honor guard. There are lots of flowers there. There again, I took out a copy of the Communist newspaper, *Pravda*, only two steps away from the soldiers. They thought I was devotedly studying Russian science. But I prayed and said to our Blessed Mother, "These soldiers are also your children. They and those flowers are here for your honor, not for this mummy of Lenin." I said the prayer for the consecration of Russia there too. While I was walking across Red Square, I prayed the Rosary and the *Veni Creator Spiritus*. At one side of the Square there was a huge building with the inscription: "Communism will triumph." "No," I said, "Christ has triumphed. He will win again through Mary!"

The next day we went to Sagorsk. Sagorsk is the spiritual center of the Orthodox Church. We were at the grave of Saint Sergius and I was very impressed. So many people prayed there. I have never experienced anything like this in my entire life: *"Gospodi pomiluj, Gospodi pomiluj!*—Lord, have mercy, have mercy, have mercy!" About one hundred times. I said to Our Lord, "You would have a stone instead of a heart, if you didn't listen to these people and answer them soon." Further I said, "You would be worse than the judge in the Gospel, who didn't care about God or the people, but finally answered the widow only to have peace. You have to answer these people, at least to have rest from them." I'm sure the victory will come soon, the answer to so many prayers. For seventy years the people of this nation have been asking for the mercy of our Lord and praying to the Blessed Mother. In no country on earth is she so loved as in Russia, and nowhere are so many hearts praying to her as in Russia. Often I have said to Satan with regard to Communism, "You made a strategic mistake when you chose Russia as the locus of the battle. Russia is the country of Our Lady. Here she is called *Bogorodica*, which means Mother of God. You will lose in Russia. Already you are on the losing side."

Yesterday I met a Russian woman. She is more than eighty years old. When I spoke to her in Russian, she began to cry. "I've lost everything, my husband, my children." Another woman told me the same thing at this church in Sagorsk. I asked her where she came from, and she told me, "From Ukraine." I asked her what she was doing. She began to cry. She didn't know that I was a bishop. I looked like a tourist. She told me that she had been carried off to Siberia. "I've lost everything. My children too. The only consolation I have is my belief in God and in the Mother of God. God can, God must help."

In a museum there was a guide who explained an icon. "That is the so-called Sad Mother of God. She is sad because she foresees that she has to offer up her child for us." She said it with such warmth that I asked myself if she said it as a mother or as a believer. Indeed, as it turned out later, she was a believer.

I came in contact with the people in Sagorsk, and I spoke with them. They asked me where I was from. "From Rome." "So? Are you a tourist from Rome, where the Pope lives?" They didn't know that I was a bishop. After that, they asked me if I was Russian Orthodox. "No, I'm a Catholic. But everybody knows that the Catholics and the Orthodox have the same faith in God and the same love of the Mother of God." "Yes, that is true, we are brothers," they replied. "Give our regards to the Holy Father." "I will do it gladly. What are you expecting from the Holy Father? What should he do for you?" And they answered spontaneously, "Bibles! Bibles! We need Bibles, but in our language. Tell the Holy Father he should provide us with Bibles." When I told this to the Holy Father, he had tears in his eyes. "You see, they don't ask for gold, silver, money— not even for bread—but for the Word of God. We must give it to them." They need millions of Bibles. This request is addressed to all Catholics, for every brother is without a Gospel, without a Bible. That is a contribution to the triumph of Mary in Russia

Once, after a homily about Fatima I gave in the Church of Saint Mary Major, I spoke with a woman who had been paralyzed for thirty years. She couldn't even eat alone. I asked her, "Would you like to offer it up for Brezhnev?" In those days he was the General Secretary of the Communist Party. She answered, "For anyone else, but not for that gangster!" I said to her, "Easy, easy. You can say that to me, but if the Mother of God asked for this sacrifice, what would you say?" "Oh yes, I couldn't say no to our Lady."

A short time ago a Russian doctor—a military doctor with the rank of colonel—came to Czechoslovakia. A nurse, who is a religious sister, but can only disclose her identity as a nurse, gave him a Bible. He kissed it and pressed it to his heart and said with tears, "This is the most beautiful present you could give me. Unfortunately, when I go to Russia, I will have to tear it into hundreds of pieces to give to others who will then copy them."

We can help them. Every Gospel produces new Christians. That is an apostolate. But we are able to do this only if we apply ourselves and make sacrifices. A widow wrote to me, "I've lost my husband, and I want to offer some money for the conversion of Russia." A mother wrote to me, "I've lost a child.

I offer it for the conversion of the Godless." A blind woman said, "I offer my blindness, that they will receive light."

If everybody could donate at least enough for one Bible! It costs about six dollars, the bigger ones perhaps twelve dollars. This much most people can spare. When I speak about this to the children, I say, "You shouldn't ask your mother for the money for a Gospel for a child in Russia or in Czechoslovakia. You yourself have to sacrifice ice cream or chocolate." The children write to me, "Father Paul, I gave up ten portions of ice cream. I've given up chocolate. Here is the money." Some of the children came to evening Mass recently and brought their money in boxes to the church. I asked one of them, "How much is in here?" One box had about sixty-five dollars, another one about ninety dollars.

You should have seen those children's eyes, how they lit up! They wanted to buy something nice for themselves, but they gave it up. The joy of those children was never greater than on that day.

Children have to be educated to make sacrifices. But adults can make sacrifices too. Perhaps a cigarette a day. Once I gave a homily in Sardinia in the morning, and in the evening people came into the sacristy to give me something. One woman gave me an envelope with 400,000 lire—about 350 dollars. I didn't want to take it, but the parish priest said, "Don't worry, take it, she will be happy." The woman said, "Dear Bishop, I have a small pension every month. It amounts to 270,000 lire (about 250 dollars). Actually I am saving this money for my youngest grandchild. After my death the child will inherit this sum. But during your homily I thought to myself, If I offer the money for the kingdom of God, God can take care of the child better than I." How clever this woman is; that's real wisdom. Truly, the Lord can take better care of us. We have to trust more in Him. Another woman had saved up about fourteen hundred dollars for her funeral. During the homily she thought, "I can earn for myself the kingdom of God if I sacrifice it. And that's more than a beautiful funeral with flowers and music." This again is prudence, wisdom. Everybody is able to offer sacrifices, not only with money, but also with prayer.

And one last example. When I was in Russia in the museum where the famous painting of the Trinity by Andrej Rubljow, and the most beautiful of all Marian Icons—the *Wladimirskaja*—are kept, I saw another impressive painting. It describes a scene in the history of Russia. On one side you see the invasion of the Mongolians into Russia. They murder women and children and set the churches on fire. All the people were running away. At the other side of the painting is a big church with many windows and doors. In the middle there is the Mother of God, who activated all the saints in heaven and on earth to come to the aid of Russia. You see the emperor Constantine with the inscription "In this sign you will triumph." You see the Archangel Saint Michael with his sword and many saints who want to save

Russia. History says that the Blessed Mother saved Russia in those times. But even more difficult times would come, and once more she would save Russia. As I stood before this painting, a class of children came past. They were about ten to twelve years old. Their teacher told them the story. A time would come even more grave than the time of the Mongol invasion. But the *Bogorodica*—the Blessed Mother—would save Russia.

Let's return to the message of Fatima. What does it mean? It means the activation of the powers of Heaven. All of Heaven takes part in achieving that victory, all the saints, all the angels, and the Blessed Mother. In Heaven the Mother of God does not have to ask, as we heard yesterday when she said to Bernadette: "Be so kind as to pray the Rosary." There is great joy among all the saints in Heaven when they can participate in the triumph of the Blessed Mother. She asks us for prayers and sacrifices too. Therefore we are called children of Mary. But have we really earned this name? The message of Fatima is the activation of all powers. Didn't Hitler command the general mobilization of Germany in 1939? Well, the Mother of God did the same, and she did it at Fatima. She is the co-redemptrix. She calls us to this co-redemption, to pray for it, to believe, to hope, and to love God for all those who do not love Him, for all those who most need the mercy of God.

The Holy Father said the same. If the mother country is in danger, defense is of the first priority.

All else is secondary, because the enemy wants to destroy everything. It is the same in our case. Everything else should be put aside so we can convert Russia. Through us the Blessed Mother has to become co-redemptrix for our brothers. That's right! We too are to be co-redeemers for our brothers. I make up in my body what is lacking in the sufferings of Christ.

The Blessed Mother calls us to the highest career possible—to become co-redeemers for our brothers in Christ. That is the meaning of the message of Fatima, the message of peace. We shouldn't ask only, but we should also apply ourselves with all our hearts. Pope Paul VI wrote the encyclical *Signum Magnum*—the Great Sign—the sign of the end, the triumph of Mary. He wrote it in 1967, for the fiftieth anniversary of Fatima. We live in the last times. We are all signs, a sign of Mary or a sign of Satan.

God said to Satan, "I will put enmity between you and the woman, and between your offspring and hers" (Gen 3:15). We are standing on the side of Mary. Let us prepare through prayer and sacrifice, especially, for the conversion of Russia! There are some other intentions we might put aside for a time, for example, the souls in Purgatory. Ninety-nine percent of the Holy Masses are offered for those who are already saved. The Poor Souls are already saved—but I am not saved yet. I can still be lost, but they are guaranteed Heaven. Let us pray and sacrifice for those who most need the mercy of

God, the Godless. On the anniversaries of our deceased we could also offer Holy Mass for this intention. My mother, who is in Heaven or in Purgatory, will be happy if I offer my Mass for those who most need the mercy of God. We have to help the Poor Souls, that's true, but even more, the poor sinners. That's how Mary wants it. She showed Hell to the children at Fatima, where so many sinners go because nobody prays for them. She tells us that there are so few who pray for them. She has compassion on them. "In order to save these souls," she says, "God,"—God wants it, not Mary!—"wants the devotion to my Immaculate Heart."

On the fiftieth anniversary of Fatima, Pope Paul VI quoted St. Ambrose: "May the Heart of Mary be found in every Christian, so that every Christian can say the *Magnificat*, 'My soul magnifies the Lord,' and also the *Fiat*, 'Your will be done.'" We are called to co-redemption. That's the message of Fatima.

Now let us intercede in this Holy Mass for those who most need the mercy of God.

Praised be Jesus Christ+

(Readers who wish to contact Bishop Hnilica may write to him at Pro Fratribus, Casella Postale 6245, 00195 Rome, Italy.)

7

POPE JOHN PAUL II'S TEACHING ON FATIMA 1982–1991

LOOKING BACK OVER THE DECADE 1981–91, it is clear that under Pope John Paul II, Fatima has providentially developed into a new and significantly deeper dimension in the life of the Church. In the general audience of May 15, 1991, on his return to Rome from Portugal, the Holy Father himself stated: *"I consider this entire decade to be a free gift, given to me in a .special way by Divine Providence* (my emphasis). A special responsibility was given to me that I might continue to serve the Church by exercising the ministry of Peter."

In this chapter, I want to consider briefly the Holy Father's teaching on the meaning of Fatima and its application to the Church today. John Paul II's first pronouncement on Fatima was his homily in May 1982, which contains a profound exposition of the whole *raison d'etre* of Fatima, and of the significance of Mary's Motherhood in the life of the Church. In it he sets out his main themes, listed under the headings below, which explain why the message of Fatima "is still more relevant than it was sixty-five years ago . . . still more urgent." As I show, the Holy Father returned to the same themes, in slightly different terms, in his addresses at Fatima in May 1991. All the words quoted from the Holy Father in these addresses are taken from the English edition of *L'Osservatore Romano* for May 20, 1991. The headings are my own.

The Message of Fatima is a call to repent and believe in the Gospel

In his 1982 homily, John Paul II says: "If the Church has accepted the Message of Fatima, it is above all because that message contains a truth and a call whose basic content is the truth and the call of the Gospel itself. 'Repent and believe in the Gospel' (Mk 1:15). These are the first words that the Messiah addressed to humanity. The Message of Fatima is, in its basic nucleus, a call to conversion and repentance, as in the Gospel . . . The appeal of the Lady of the Message of Fatima is so deeply rooted in the Gospel and the whole of Tradition, that the Church feels that *the message imposes a commitment on her. . . .*" (my emphasis).

In his general audience of May 15, 1991, the Holy Father repeated the above definition, that Our Lord's words in Mark 1:15 constitute a synthesis of Mary's message at Fatima, and then went on to state: "The events which have taken place on our European continent, particularly in Central and Eastern Europe, give this Gospel appeal a contemporary meaning on the threshold of the third millennium. *These events compel us in a special way to think about Fatima* (emphasis in the original). The heart of the Mother of God is the heart of a Mother who cares not only for individuals, but for entire peoples and nations. This heart is totally dedicated to the saving mission of her Son: Christ, the Redeemer of the world, the Redeemer of man. . . ." And at the candle-light prayer vigil at Fatima on May 12, the Pope stated: "In its message and blessing, Fatima means conversion to God. In this place we feel and are witness to the redemption of mankind through the intercession and with the help of her whose virginal feet have always and will continue to crush the head of the ancient serpent."

Sin and the denial of God

In his 1982 homily, the Holy Father describes how "sin has made itself firmly at home in the world, and denial of God has become widespread in the ideologies, ideas and plans of human beings. . . ." The Holy Father openly confesses that he reads again "with trepidation the motherly call to penance, to conversion, the ardent appeal of the Heart of Mary that resounded at Fatima sixty-five years ago . . . because he sees how many people and societies—how many

Christians—*have gone in the opposite direction to the one indicated in the Message of Fatima* (my emphasis). "In the light of a mother's love," he continues, "we understand the whole message of the Lady of Fatima. The greatest obstacle to man's journey towards God is sin, perseverance in sin, and finally, denial of God. The deliberate blotting out of God from the world of human thought. The detachment from Him of the whole of man's earthly activity. The rejection of God by man..." It is precisely for this reason, the Holy Father observes, that "the evangelical call to repentance and conversion, uttered in the Mother's message, remains ... still more relevant ... still more urgent."

In his general audience of May 15, 1991, the Holy Father said that his visit to Fatima had been not only an occasion for thanksgiving, but also "... one of *intense supplication.* This is because the hands on the clock of time are moving toward the year 2000, and they show not only the providential changes in the history of entire nations, but also *old and new threats...* In the *liturgy of Fatima,* the book of Revelation shows us not only a "woman clothed with the sun" (Rev 12:1), but the same woman also shares all the mortal threats against her children to whom she gives birth in pain. This is because *the Mother of God,* as the last Council recalled, *is the model of the Church-Mother.* Mother of the Church, your servant on the chair of Peter thanks you for all the good which transforms the face of the earth, in spite of so many threats...." (Words emphasized as in the original).

It is clear that the Holy Father has come to regard the prevailing spirit of Godlessness as the most serious of the disorders afflicting modern society, since he issues graphic warnings against this cardinal sin in all three of his addresses at Fatima in 1991. At the candlelight vigil of May 12, he recognized that "Our Lady has been the pledge *par excellence* of their fidelity and the certitude of salvation . . . for the great multitude of believers who have been so sorely tried by difficulties . . . and who, often even in persecution and suffering, have been faithful to God, with their hearts and eyes turned to the Virgin Mary . . . Dear Mother," he says, towards the end of this homily, *"help us in this godless desert in which our generation and that of our children seems to be lost* (my emphasis). May they finally rediscover the divine well-springs of their own life and rest there." He is well aware that the Godless spirit behind Communism is not dead, and so warns of "the danger of replacing Marxism with another form of atheism which, praising freedom, tends to destroy the roots of human and Christian morality" (Act of Entrustment). He told the Portuguese episcopal conference that the European continent is troubled "by a broad theoretical and practical atheism which seems to want to build a new materialistic civilization."

His strongest denunciation of this grave threat to the faith came during his homily on the feast of Our Lady of Fatima: "In these men and women of the twentieth century we have seen both the capacity to subjugate the earth, and the freedom to escape the law of God and deny it, as the inheritance of sin. The inheritance of sin shows itself as an *insane aspiration to build the world*—a world created by humanity—*as if God did not exist* (my emphasis). And also as if there were no cross on Golgotha. . . ."

The universality of Mary's message

"The message is addressed to every human being," John Paul II says, in his homily of 1982. "The love of the Savior's Mother reaches every place touched by the work of salvation. Her care extends to every individual of our time, and to all societies, nations and peoples. Societies menaced by apostasy, threatened by moral degradation. The collapse of morality involves the collapse of societies . . . Can the Mother who, with all the force of the love that she fosters in the Holy Spirit, desires everyone's salvation, keep silence on what undermines the very bases of their salvation? No, she cannot."

Ten years later the Holy Father repeats this teaching in a different form, in his special Act of Entrustment at Fatima in May 1991, which is a veritable litany of invocations to Our Lady on behalf of every human state and need in the world. "Continue to show yourself a mother to everyone," he invokes her, "because the world needs you . . . Today I renew the filial entrustment of the human race to you. With confidence we entrust everyone to you . . . Mary, Mother of the Redeemer, continue to show yourself Mother of all."

In his homily on the feast of Our Lady of Fatima, he said: "Mary, who was near the Cross of her Son, had to accept one more time the will of Christ, Son of God. But while on Golgotha the Son pointed out one man only, John, the beloved disciple, she has had to receive everyone—all of us, the men and women of this century and of its difficult and dramatic history... Your universal motherhood, O Virgin Mary," he says, at the end of this powerful homily, "is the sure anchor of salvation for the whole of humankind. Mother of the Redeemer! Full of grace! I salute you, Mother, trust of all generations!"

Mary's appeal is from generation to generation

"Mary's appeal is not just for once," said the Holy Father in 1982. "Her appeal must be taken up by generation after generation, in accordance with the ever new 'signs of the times.' It must be unceasingly returned to. It must be ever taken up anew."

At the candle-light vigil in May 1991, the Holy Father said that "the Church, for her part, does not cease consecrating herself to Mary . . . whose virginal feet have always and will continue to crush the head of the ancient serpent." His special Act of Entrustment invoked the presence and protection of Mary in every human state and need, now and forward into the future; and he seemed to sum up this teaching when he stated, at the end of his homily: "Always and now, you watch with the greatest motherly care, defending with your powerful intercession the dawn of Christ's light in the midst of peoples and nations. Always and forever you remain, because the only Son of God, your Son, entrusted all humanity to you when, dying on the Cross, he brought us into the new beginning of everything which exists. . . ."

The Pope explains the significance of Fatima for the Church

There are three other features in John Paul II's addresses on his visit to Fatima in May 1991 which indicate the significance the Holy Father attaches to the message of Fatima for the Church, as it looks forward to the third millennium.

Firstly, in his opening homily from the Capelinha at the candle-light prayer vigil on May 12, the Pope recalled the Act of Consecration which he had carried out in Rome on March 25, 1984: "On that memorable day . . . you, holy Mother, granted us the grace of visiting our *house*, St. Peter's Basilica, so that we could place in your Immaculate Heart our Act of Consecration of the world . . . Today . . . I have come to your *throne* (my emphasis) to acclaim you: Hail, Holy Mother! Hail, sure hope which never disappoints! *Totus tuus*, O Mother! Thank you, heavenly Mother, for having guided people to freedom with your motherly affection."

The Pope is talking to Our Lady, in that simple, direct manner one observes of him at certain moments. It is she, he says, who granted the Vicar of

Christ the grace of traveling from the Capelinha at Fatima to visit him at St. Peter's Basilica; and in recognition of her dignity as Queen of Heaven, John Paul II describes her seat at Fatima as a throne, a place specially chosen and favored by God, in contrast to his own simple house of St. Peter's. There is a courteous respect in these carefully chosen words, and by this reference, the Holy Father might also have had in mind the crowning of the Pilgrim Virgin statue at Fatima as Queen of the World, which had been carried out by Cardinal Masella, legate of Pope Pius XII, on May 13, 1946. Now, forty-five years later, there had been placed inside that same crown, worn by the Queen of Heaven on her throne at Fatima, one of the bullets which had been fired at John Paul II outside his house of St. Peter's Basilica.

Secondly, during this visit to Fatima, the Holy Father made a special Act of Entrustment to the Mother of the Redeemer (printed in full in Appendix V), which is a moving testimony of his simple devotion to and trust in Mary's powerful presence and intercession. It is a veritable litany of invocations to Our Lady on behalf of every human need and condition, and as such is a model and an example to be imitated.

"How many times we have invoked you! And today we are here to thank you because you always listened to us . . . to thank you for what you have done in these difficult years for the Church, for each of us, for all humanity." The Pope begins by thanking her for showing herself a Mother: Mother of the Church, Mother of all people, Mother of the Nations "by the

Pope John Paul II at Fatima, May 1991

unexpected changes which restored confidence to peoples who were oppressed and humiliated for so long . . . My Mother for ever, and especially on May 13, 1981, when I felt your helpful presence at my side." The Pope opens his heart to Mary, he tells her everything. It is visible, in this Act of Entrustment. He knows well that "the new conditions of peoples and the Church are still precarious and unstable," and so he implores Mary to show herself a Mother to everyone, "because the world needs you." He is aware that the spirit behind Communism is not dead, and hence warns of "the danger of replacing Marxism with another form of atheism which, praising freedom, tends to destroy the roots of human and Christian morality."

There is need for Mary, he continues, "in the nations which recently acquired room for freedom and are now committed to building their future. There is need for you in Europe, which from East to West cannot reclaim its true identity without discovering its common Christian roots. Watch over the leaders of the nations," he calls upon Mary, "and those who influence the fate of humanity. Watch over the Church, which is always threatened by the spirit of the world." Every human need and state he confides to her, simply, trustingly, without reserve, and that is why, as he says, she always listens to him. The whole of this Act is an inspiring example of how authentic devotion to Our Lady is intensely practical in nature. In summary, it is both a meditation on the present state of the world, and a renewal of John Paul II's confident, filial entrustment of the whole human race to the "Mother of hope . . . Mother of the Nations," imploring Mary to "walk with us along this last furrow of the twentieth century . . . watch over the road which still awaits us."

Lastly, in his homily on the feast of Our Lady of Fatima, as a commentary on the words of the Man of Sorrows to his Mother at the foot of the Cross, the Holy Father presented an eschatological survey of human history. "The sanctuary of Fatima," he went on to state, "is a privileged place endowed with a special value: it contains in itself an important message for the era in which we are living . . . I, a pilgrim with you in this new Jerusalem, exhort you, dear brothers and sisters, to accept the grace and the appeal which in this place is felt so palpably, so penetratingly, in the sense of turning your ways to the ways of God. . . ." Earlier in the same homily, he stated, "in the center of this history of humanity and of the world, the Cross of Christ is raised up over Golgotha. . . ." Towards the end, he returned to the scene of the Crucifixion in a phrase which links Fatima in history with the very origins of the Church. Commenting on the words: "Woman, behold your son, son, behold your Mother," he stated: *"It is as if here, at the beginning of our century, the words pronounced on Golgotha re-echoed anew"* (my emphasis).

8

CONCLUSION

I BEGAN TO WRITE THIS STUDY in September 1991. The astonishing changes that were in progress at that time continued until the very last days of the year, and brought with them the definitive conclusion to two distinct but related themes which have been central to this work.

In the first place, on Christmas Day 1991 the existence of the Soviet Union was formally terminated when President Mikhail Gorbachev resigned. Henceforward, there was nothing to stand in the path of the former Soviet Union's republics, and the realization of the new political era towards which they have been striving.

And secondly, on October 13, 1991, for the first time since Our Lady had appeared in 1917 to ask for the consecration of Russia, the ceremonies in Fatima were attended by pilgrims from Russia and, by permission of President Yeltsin, live television coverage of this event was shown in Moscow and all over the Soviet Union. This pilgrimage aptly symbolized in general the ending of the religious persecution of Christians in the countries in Central and Eastern Europe under Soviet domination, and in particular, the conclusion of the long period of separation from the life of the Church which Catholics in those countries have suffered in this century.

These two events clearly demonstrate that freedom of thought and action, in people's political and religious life, has now been recognized and enacted in place of the Marxist totalitarian tyranny on which the former Soviet Union was founded, and this is probably the single most important consequence of its demise. For it was the forcible restraint of individual freedom, and the straitjacket imposed on people's thoughts and actions by the erroneous and inhuman ideology of the previous regime, which has been the prime cause of the grave and urgent problems—spiritual, moral and material—now facing those peoples. To his credit, President Gorbachev freely and honestly admitted this in his speech of resignation.

More importantly, for the first time since the 1917 Revolution, when the state began its campaign of opposition and hostility against it, the Church has now recovered the freedom to pursue her mission of working for the return of society to God. Of all the gains to have accrued from the changes that have taken place, this is the most significant, for only the Church, out of her divine mission and infinite spiritual resources, can restore the moral fibre and purpose of a society that has been almost completely severed from its spiritual foundations.

Until the iron grip of Marxism's all-embracing domination over people's lives began to be loosed from within, for Christians there was only a very hard winter to be endured with no hope of spring, as Cardinal Casaroli remarked after President Gorbachev's visit to the Holy Father on December 1, 1989. But now that the totalitarian tyranny has been broken and discarded, springtime has come, and the Church in Central and Eastern Europe finds herself free once more to preach anew to modern man Our Lord's invitation, delivered at the opening of the first millennium, to "repent and believe in the Gospel" (Mk 1:15). The same call to conversion and repentance, as John Paul II said in his homily of May 1982, is the basic nucleus of the message which the Savior's Virgin Mother communicated at Fatima in this, the last century of the second millennium. For the first time in many years, those countries are now also open to hear Mary's consoling message of warning and hope, and to learn of its special significance for them. By a design of Providence, the message of Fatima was given a spectacular launch in the Soviet Union on October 13, 1991, when a seventy-five-minute broadcast of the ceremonies, on the occasion of the first Russian pilgrimage ever to be received at Fatima, was transmitted live on television to Moscow and seen by between thirty and forty million people. The broadcast was so popular that it was shown again on November 7, the day on which, in every preceding year, a military parade had always been held in Moscow's Red Square to celebrate the 1917 atheist Revolution.

With the collapse of the former tyranny, it also follows that for the first time Russia has become open to the conversion that Mary promised will come "in the end" through her Immaculate Heart. However, marvelous though all these recent events are, and full of promise and hope for the future, it is clear that they only represent a first step in the direction of Russia's eventual conversion that Our Lady intends. By that conversion, Mary surely means a general turning toward and acceptance of God by the peoples of Russia, and it is hardly surprising, given the appalling legacy of suffering and chaos bequeathed by the previous regime, that this has not yet taken place. Humanly speaking, it will obviously take time before the Church can regain her position in society and thereby contribute to bringing that desirable outcome to pass. Meanwhile, it is evident that the recent events form the indispensable first step in the process of conversion, in the sense of a determined rejection of the evil of the previous regime by the peoples of Russia. It was the work of Mikhail Gorbachev that enabled this to happen by loosing the iron grip of Marxism's all-embracing domination over people's lives. And this step itself was made possible by Pope John Paul II's consecration of the world to Mary's Immaculate Heart on March 25, 1984.

What has happened, therefore, is of deep significance in the history of the Fatima revelations, and it marks a major development in the progress of Our Lady's message in the life of the Church. This study begins with the intervention of Mary to save the life of John Paul II on the feast of Our Lady of Fatima, May 13, 1981. It ends with the collapse of the coup against President Gorbachev on the feast of the Queenship of Mary, August 22, 1991; with the founding of a commonwealth by the three leading republics on the feast of the Immaculate Conception on December 8; with the announcement, on the same day, that the Soviet Union was dead; and with the final dissolution of the Soviet Union by President Gorbachev on the feast of the Nativity of Our Lord. Thus the beginning and the end of the whole remarkable process of transformation was heralded by the discreet but powerful presence and intervention of Mary. The key operative factor, however, which Heaven waited to be fulfilled, was the consecration of Russia to the Immaculate Heart of Mary that the Holy Father duly performed in March 1984. Here, too, the presence of Mary may be discerned, for it was while John Paul II was in the hospital in 1981 that he sent for all the Fatima documentation, studied it with extreme attention, and as a result came to understand that "the only way to save the world from war, to save it from atheism, is the conversion of Russia according to the message of Fatima."

Prior to March 1984, both Pius XII and Paul VI had made consecrations to Mary's Immaculate Heart, and clearly these were acceptable and pleasing to Almighty God. Nevertheless, history records that despite these acts, the malign power of the former Soviet Union continued to increase, threatening the peace

and stability of the whole world with its wars and persecutions of the Church, as Our Lady of Fatima had
forewarned. John Paul II's words rang deep and true
when he told the Church, in his homily at Fatima in
May 1982: "My heart is oppressed when I see the sin
of the world and the whole range of menaces gathering like a dark cloud over mankind."

One can understand that the Holy Father felt oppressed at this prospect, but he was not cast down, for
he knew that to counter this grave situation, God had
provided the remedy which he annunciated in his
very next words: "But it (my heart) also rejoices with
hope as I once more do what has been done by my
predecessors, when they consecrated the world to the
heart of the Mother . . . Doing this means consecrating
the world to Him who is infinite holiness. This holiness means redemption. *It means a love more powerful
than evil. No 'sin of the world' can ever overcome this love"*
(my emphasis). Only a few years later, those words of
the Holy Father found a marvelous fulfillment when,
on Christmas Day 1991, President Gorbachev peacefully declared that the Soviet Union, the personifica-
tion of the Marxist 'sin of the world,' no longer
existed. Some three months after that, in March 1992,
Mr. Gorbachev published an article, in the regular column which he has recently begun to write for *La
Stampa* in Italy, in which he publicly thanked John
Paul II for the Pope's crucial role in bringing about the
changes in Eastern Europe. These events, said Mr.
Gorbachev, "could not have happened without the
presence of this Pope." That is a remarkable tribute,

but even more significant, in the context of the interaction of the supernatural that has been the theme of this study, is the disclosure Mr. Gorbachev made about his relationship with the Holy Father: "There is a deep sense of sympathy and mutual understanding between us . . . *I always appreciate above all the spiritual content of the Pope's thinking*" (my emphasis).

Developments have succeeded each other with extraordinary rapidity in recent months, and in consequence attention is now almost exclusively focused on the enormous problems left behind by the collapse of the former USSR. In order to appreciate the magnitude of what has taken place, it is necessary to cast one's mind back to 1982, when the Holy Father spoke the words I have just quoted. At that time, the whole situation was so different, could anyone have imagined that such an almost unbelievable demise was possible, let alone imminent, within less than a single decade?

No one could possibly have foreseen in what way Heaven was going to respond to John Paul II's consecration, but when one considers the extraordinary manner in which events unfolded after March 25, 1984, as I have sought to demonstrate in this work, then can it be doubted that what we have witnessed is an intervention by Almighty God, in response to the intercession of Our Lady of Fatima, now that her request for the consecration of Russia had been fulfilled?

It is for the reader to make up his own mind in response to this question. All that I have sought to do is to set out the evidence which in my belief justifies this conclusion. At the heart of the Revolution to which Russia succumbed in 1917 was that sin, described by John Paul II in his homily of May 1982 as man's greatest obstacle in his journey towards God, namely, "the denial of God. The deliberate blotting out of God from the world of man's earthly activity. The rejection of God by man." That gravely distorted ideology dominated every aspect of life in the former USSR, to the extent that if one omits or discounts its influence, it then becomes impossible to arrive at a correct understanding of all the other social, political and economic factors which have also been at work.

It is my contention that only the supernatural intervention briefly depicted in this study affords a credible explanation of how such a regime, motivated by such open and unrelenting opposition to God and the Church, could come to turn about upon its original principles and purpose. It did this of its own volition, peacefully from within, abandoning its campaign of spiritual warfare against the Church and voting itself out of existence.

Finally, it is my hope that readers of this book will be moved by the extraordinary unfolding of events in this past decade to pray and meditate deeply on the divine mysteries of which they are the manifestation. May they be encouraged to comply with generosity in their personal lives to the simple requests of Our Lady of Fatima, following the example of our Holy Father, John Paul II.

As we reflect on the *magnalia Dei*—the great works of God—that have taken place, our generation can indeed say, in the words of St. Bernard's *Memorare*, that it was never known that anyone ever fled to the protection of our most gracious Virgin Mary, implored her help, or sought her intercession and was left unaided. For we are truly witnesses that the Holy Mother of God has turned her eyes of mercy toward us, and hence that "He who is mighty has done great things to me, and holy is His name," as she herself sings in her sublime canticle of praise to Almighty God, the *Magnificat*.

APPENDIX I

CONSECRATION OF THE WORLD TO THE IMMACULATE HEART OF MARY BY POPE PIUS XII, OCTOBER 31, 1942

QUEEN OF THE MOST HOLY ROSARY, Help of Christians, Refuge of the human race, victorious in all God's battles, behold us who pray to you, kneeling before your throne, trusting that we shall obtain mercy and receive grace and timely aid in the midst of the present calamities, not because of our merits, but solely because of the immense goodness of your maternal heart. It is to you, to your Immaculate Heart, that We, as common father of the great Christian family, as Vicar of Him to whom all power in Heaven and on earth has been given, and who has entrusted us with the care of all the souls bought by His Blood who people the entire universe, it is to You, it is to your Immaculate Heart, in this tragic hour in the history of humanity, that we entrust, we give, we consecrate, not only the Holy Church, the Mystical Body of your Son

Jesus, which suffers and sheds its blood in so many places, in the midst of such tribulations, but also the whole world, torn by mortal strife, on fire with hatred, and the victim of its own evil doing.

Let your Heart be moved by the sight of such material and moral ruin, by the sorrow and anxiety of so many fathers and mothers, wives, brothers, and innocent children; by so many lives cut short in their prime; by so many bodies pulverized in horrible massacres; by so many souls tortured and in the throes of death; by so many others in danger of losing eternal life.

O Mother of Mercy, obtain for us peace from God, and first of all, those graces which can convert the hearts of men in a moment, the graces which prepare, facilitate and assure peace! Queen of Peace, pray for us, and give to the world at war the peace for which people long, peace in the truth, the justice and the charity of Christ! Give the world peace from strife and peace of soul, so that the Kingdom of God may spread in tranquillity of order. Extend your protection to unbelievers and all those who still lie in the shadow of death! Give them peace, and may the Sun of Truth shine on them too, so that they may repeat with us, before the sole Savior of the world: "Glory to God in the highest, and peace on earth to men of good will" (Lk. 2:14).

To those peoples separated from us by error or schism, and above all to those who show a special devotion to you, and in whose lands there was not a house that did not honor your venerable icon—

though now perhaps hidden and put away for better days—give peace and lead them back to the one fold of Christ, under the one true Shepherd. Obtain for the holy Church of God complete peace and freedom; stem the flood of the new paganism and materialism; foster in the hearts of the faithful the love of purity, the practice of the Christian way of life and apostolic zeal, so that the number of God's servants may grow and their merits increase.

And lastly, just as the Church and the whole human race was consecrated to the Heart of your Son Jesus, so that His Heart became for those who trusted in Him "a sign and assurance of victory and salvation" (Leo XIII, *Annum Sacrum*, May 25, 1899); so now we consecrate ourselves for ever, O Mother of us all and Queen of the world, to your Immaculate Heart, so that your love and protection may hasten the triumph of God's Kingdom, and all nations, at peace with one another and with God, may call you Blessed and sing with you, from one end of the world to another, the eternal *Magnificat* of praise, love and gratitude to the Heart of Jesus, in whom alone we may find Truth, Life and Peace."

Rome, October 31, 1942

APPENDIX II

EXTRACTS FROM
THE APOSTOLIC LETTER
OF POPE PIUS XII
TO THE PEOPLES OF RUSSIA,
"SACRO VERGENTE ANNO,"
JULY 7, 1952

DEAR PEOPLES OF RUSSIA, health and peace in
the Lord!

While the Holy Year (1950) was coming to a
happy conclusion, and after it had been given to us by
a divine disposition to solemnly define (on November
1, 1950) the dogma of the Assumption into Heaven,
body and soul, of the Holy Mother of God, the Virgin
Mary, numerous people from all parts of the world expressed their most lively joy to us; many of them,
while sending us letters of gratitude, earnestly implored us to consecrate to the Immaculate Heart of the
Virgin Mary the entire Russian people which today is
undergoing such suffering.

This supplication was most agreeable to us, for if
our paternal affection embraces all peoples, it is addressed in a particular manner to those who, although

for the most part separated from the Apostolic See by the vicissitudes of history, nevertheless still retain the name Christian, but find themselves in conditions in which it is very difficult for them to hear our voice and to know the teaching of Catholic doctrine, and in which they are even incited by deceitful and pernicious means to reject faith itself and even the very idea of God. . . .

Without doubt we have condemned and rejected —as the duty of our office demands—the errors which the instigators of atheistic Communism teach or strive to propagate for the greatest wrong and harm of the citizens . . . we have unmasked their falsehoods, which are often disguised as the truth, because we love you with the heart of a father and we wish your good . . .

We know, and that is a great hope and consolation for us, that you love and honor the Virgin Mary Mother of God with ardent affection, and that you venerate her images. We know that in the city of Moscow itself, a temple has been built—alas, withdrawn from divine worship—which is dedicated to the Assumption of the Blessed Virgin Mary into heaven; and this is a most clear testimony of the love which your forebears and you yourselves have for the Most Holy Mother of God.

Now we are well aware that the hope of Salvation can never fail wherever the Most Holy Mother of God is venerated with sincere and ardent piety. Even though powerful and cruel men may strive to uproot holy religion and Christian virtue from the souls of their fellow citizens; even though Satan himself may seek by every means to foster this sacrilegious struggle, as the Apostle of the gentiles says: ". . . for our wrestling is not against flesh and blood, but against principalities and powers, against the rulers of this world of darkness, against the spirits of wickedness in high places . . ." (Eph. 6:12); nevertheless, if Mary opposes them with her protection, the gates of hell cannot prevail. She is the most loving and all-powerful Mother of God and of all men, and never has it been heard that anyone had recourse to her with confident entreaty, and has not experienced the support of her protection. Continue then, as you are doing, to pray to her with devotion, to love her ardently, and to invoke her with these words which it is your custom to say: "To you alone has it been given to have your petitions always answered, O most holy and most pure Mother of God" (*Acath. Festi Patrocinii SS. Genetricis*, K. 3).

May the well-beloved Mother deign to look with goodness and mercy on those who organize groups of militant atheists and direct their activities; may she fill their minds with heavenly light and, by divine grace, turn their hearts towards salvation.

And so that our fervent prayers and yours may be the more readily answered, and to give you a special sign of our particular affection, just as a few years ago we consecrated the entire human race to the Immaculate Heart of the Virgin Mary, Mother of God, so now today we consecrate and we dedicate in a very special way all the peoples of Russia to this Immaculate Heart, with the firm hope that through the all-powerful protection of the Virgin Mary, there may soon be happily realized the desires which we share with you and all men of good will, for true peace, fraternal concord and liberty which is the right of all, and in the first place, of the Church. Thus, through our prayers, united with yours and those of all the Christian people, there will be firmly established throughout the world the Kingdom of the Savior Jesus Christ: "the Kingdom of truth and life, the Kingdom of sanctity and grace, the Kingdom of justice, love and peace" (Preface of Christ the King).

And we address our supplications to this most merciful Mother, that she may obtain from her divine Son heavenly light for your minds, and for your souls, the supernatural strength and courage which will enable you to avert and overcome all error and godlessness.

Rome, July 7, 1952

APPENDIX III

HOMILY OF POPE JOHN PAUL II AT FATIMA, MAY 13, 1982

(The sub-headings have been added to the original.)

1. "And from that hour the disciple took her to his own home" (Jn. 19:27).

These are the concluding words of the Gospel in today's liturgy at Fatima. The disciple's name was John. It was he, John the son of Zebedee, the Apostle and Evangelist, who heard from the Cross the words of Christ: "Behold your mother." But first Christ had said to His Mother, "Woman, behold your son." This was a wonderful testament.

As He left this world, Christ gave to His Mother a man, a human being, to be like a son for her: John. He entrusted him to her. And, as a consequence of this giving and entrusting, Mary became the mother of John. The Mother of God became the Mother of man.

From that hour, John "took her to his own home" and became the earthly guardian of the Mother of his Master; for sons have the right and duty to care for their mother. John became by Christ's will the son of the Mother of God. And in John every human being became her child.

The Mother's presence in the world

2. The words "he took her to his own home" can be taken in the literal sense as referring to the place where he lived. Mary's motherhood in our regard is manifested in a particular way in the places where she meets us: her dwelling places; places in which a special presence of the Mother is felt.

There are many such dwelling places. They are of all kinds; from a special corner in the home or little wayside shrines adorned with an image of the Mother of God, to chapels and churches built in her honor. However, in certain places the Mother's presence is felt in a particularly vivid way. These places sometimes radiate their light over a great distance and draw people from afar. Their radiance may extend over a diocese, a whole nation, or at times over several countries and even continents. These places are the Marian sanctuaries or shrines.

In all these places that unique testament of the Crucified Lord is wonderfully actualized: in them man feels that he is entrusted and confided to Mary; he goes there in order to be with her, as with his Mother; he opens his heart to her and speaks to her about everything; he "takes her to his own home," that is to say, he brings her into all his problems, which at times are difficult—his own problems and those of others; the problems of the family, of societies, of nations, and of the whole of humanity.

3. Is not this the case with the shrine at Lourdes, in France? Is not this the case with Jasna Gora, in Poland, my own country's shrine, which this year is celebrating its six hundredth anniversary? There too, as in so many other shrines of Mary throughout the world, the words of today's liturgy seem to resound with a particularly authentic force: "You are the great pride of our nation" (Judith 15:9), and also: "When our nation was brought low . . . you avenged our ruin, walking in the straight path before our God" (Judith 13:20).

At Fatima these words resound as one particular echo of the experiences, not only of the Portuguese nation, but also of so many other countries and peoples on this earth; indeed, they echo the experience of modern mankind as a whole, the whole of the human family.

John Paul II's special call to Fatima

4. And so I come here today because on this very day last year, in St. Peter's Square in Rome, the attempt on the Pope's life was made, in mysterious coincidence with the anniversary of the first apparition at Fatima, which occurred on May 13, 1917. I seemed to recognize in the coincidence of the dates a special

call to come to this place. And so, today I am here. I have come in order to thank Divine Providence in this place which the Mother of God seems to have chosen in a particular way. *"Misericordiae Domini, quia non sumus consumpti* (Through God's mercy we were spared"—Lam. 2:22), I repeat once more with the prophet.

I have come especially in order to confess here the glory of God Himself: "Blessed be the Lord God, who created the heavens and the earth," I say in the words of today's liturgy (Judith 13:18).

And to the Creator of Heaven and earth I also raise that special hymn of glory which is she herself, the Immaculate Mother of the Incarnate Word: "O daughter, you are blessed by the Most High God above all women on earth . . . your hope will never depart from the hearts of men, as they remember the power of God. May God grant this to be a perpetual honor to you" (Judith 13:24).

At the basis of this song of praise, which the Church lifts up with joy here as in so many other places on the earth, is the incomparable choice of a daughter of the human race to be the Mother of God.

And therefore let God above all be praised: Father, Son and Holy Spirit. May blessing and veneration be given to Mary, the model of the Church, as the "dwelling place of the Most Holy Trinity."

Mary's spiritual Motherhood

5. From the time when Jesus, dying on the Cross, said to John: "Behold your mother"; from the time when "the disciple took her to his own home," the mystery of the spiritual motherhood of Mary has been actualized boundlessly in history. Motherhood means caring for the life of the child. Since Mary is the Mother of us all, her care for the life of man is universal. The care of a mother embraces her child totally. Mary's motherhood has its beginning in her motherly care for Christ. In Christ, at the foot of the Cross, she accepted John, and in John she accepted all of us totally. Mary embraces us all with special solicitude in the Holy Spirit. For, as we profess in our Creed, He is "the Giver of life." It is He who gives the fullness of life, open towards eternity.

Mary's spiritual motherhood is therefore a sharing in the power of the Holy Spirit, of "the Giver of life." It is the humble service of her who says of herself: "Behold, I am the handmaid of the Lord" (Lk. 1:38).

In the light of the mystery of Mary's spiritual motherhood, let us seek to understand the extraordinary message, which began on May 13, 1917 to resound throughout the world from Fatima, continuing for five months until October 13 of the same year.

The message of Fatima is a call to convert and repent

6. The Church has always taught and continues to proclaim that God's revelation was brought to completion in Jesus Christ, who is the fullness of that revelation, and that "no new public revelation is to be expected before the glorious manifestation of Our Lord." (*Dei Verbum*, 4). The Church evaluates and judges private revelations by the criterion of conformity with that single public Revelation.

If the Church has accepted the message of Fatima, it is above all because that message contains a truth and a call whose basic content is the truth and the call of the Gospel itself. "Repent, and believe in the Gospel" (Mk. 1:15). These are the first words that the Messiah addressed to humanity. The message of Fatima is, in its basic nucleus, a call to conversion and repentance, as in the Gospel. This call was uttered at the beginning of the twentieth century, and it was thus addressed particularly to this present century. The Lady of the message seems to have read with special insight the "signs of the times," the signs of our time.

The call to repentance is a motherly one, and at the same time it is strong and decisive. The love that "rejoices in the truth" (cf. 1 Cor. 13) is capable of being clear-cut and firm. The call to repentance is linked, as always, with a call to prayer. In harmony with the tradition of many centuries, the Lady of the message indicates the Rosary, which can rightly be defined as "Mary's prayer," the prayer in which she feels particularly united with us. She herself prays with us. The Rosary prayer embraces the problems of the Church, of the See of Peter, the problems of the whole world. In it we also remember sinners, that they may be converted and saved, and the souls in Purgatory.

The words of the message were addressed to children aged from seven to ten. Children, like Bernadette of Lourdes, are particularly privileged in these apparitions of the Mother of God. Hence the fact that her language to them is also simple, within the limits of their understanding. The children of Fatima became partners in dialogue with the Lady of the message and collaborators with her. One of them is still living.

The love of the Mother for the sinner

7. When Jesus on the Cross said, "Woman, behold your son" (Jn. 19:26), in a new way He opened His Mother's heart, the Immaculate Heart, and revealed to it the new dimensions and extent of the love to which she was called in the Holy Spirit by the power of the sacrifice of the Cross.

In the words of Fatima we seem to find this dimension of motherly love, whose range covers the whole of man's path towards God; the path that leads through this world and that goes, through Purgatory, beyond this world. The solicitude of the Mother of the Savior is solicitude for the work of salvation: the work of her Son. It is solicitude for the salvation, the eternal salvation, of all. Now that sixty-five years have passed since that May 13, 1917, it is difficult to fail to notice how the range of this salvific love of the Mother embraces, in a particular way, our century.

In the light of a mother's love we understand the whole message of the Lady of Fatima. The greatest obstacle to man's journey towards God is sin, perseverance in sin, and finally, denial of God. The deliberate blotting out of God from the world of human thought. The detachment from Him of the whole of man's earthly activity. The rejection of God by man.

In reality, the eternal salvation of man is only in God. Man's rejection of God, if it becomes definitive, leads logically to God's rejection of man (cf. Mt. 7:23; 10:33), to damnation.

Can the Mother who, with all the force of the love that she fosters in the Holy Spirit, desires everyone's salvation, keep silence on what undermines the very bases of their salvation? No, she cannot.

And so, while the message of Our Lady of Fatima is a motherly one, it is also strong and decisive. It sounds severe. It sounds like John the Baptist speaking on the banks of the Jordan. It invites to repentance. It gives a warning. It calls to prayer. It recommends the Rosary. The message is addressed to every human being. The love of the Savior's Mother reaches every place touched by the work of salvation. Her care extends to every individual of our time, and to all the societies, nations and peoples. Societies menaced by apostasy, threatened by moral degradation. The collapse of morality involves the collapse of societies.

Consecration to the Heart of the Mother

8. On the Cross Christ said, "Woman, behold your son!" With these words He opened in a new way His Mother's heart. A little later, the Roman soldier's spear pierced the side of the Crucified One. That pierced heart became a sign of the redemption achieved through the death of the Lamb of God.

The Immaculate Heart of Mary, opened with the words, "Woman, behold your son!" is spiritually united with the heart of her Son, opened by the soldier's spear. Mary's heart was opened by the same love for man and for the world with which Christ loved man and the world, offering Himself for them on the Cross, until the soldier's spear struck that blow.

Consecrating the world to the Immaculate Heart of Mary means drawing near, through the Mother's intercession, to the very Fountain of life that sprang from Golgotha. This Fountain unceasingly pours forth redemption and grace. In it reparation is made continually for the sins of the world. It is a ceaseless source of new life and holiness.

Consecrating the world to the Immaculate Heart of the Mother means returning beneath the Cross of the Son. It means consecrating this world to the pierced heart of the Savior, bringing it back to the very source of its redemption. Redemption is always

greater than man's sins and the "sin of the world."
The power of the Redemption is infinitely superior to
the whole range of evil in man and in the world.

The heart of the Mother is aware of this, more
than any other heart in the whole universe, visible and
invisible. And so she calls us. She not only calls to us
to be converted; she calls us to accept her motherly
help to return to the source of redemption.

9. Consecrating ourselves to Mary means accepting her help to offer ourselves and the whole of mankind to Him who is holy, infinitely holy; it means
accepting her help—by having recourse to her motherly heart, which beneath the Cross was opened to
love for every human being, for the whole world—in
order to offer the world, the individual human being,
mankind as a whole, and all the nations, to Him who
is infinitely holy. God's holiness showed itself in the
redemption of man, of the world, of the whole of
mankind, and of the nations: a redemption brought
about through the sacrifice of the Cross. "For their
sake I consecrate myself," Jesus had said (Jn. 17:19).

By the power of the Redemption, the world and
man have been consecrated. They have been consecrated to Him who is infinitely holy. They have been
offered and entrusted to Love itself, merciful Love.

The Mother of Christ calls us, invites us to join
with the Church of the living God in the consecration
of the world, in this act of confiding by which the
world, mankind as a whole, the nations, each individual person are presented to the Eternal Father with the

power of the Redemption won by Christ. They are offered in the heart of the Redeemer which was pierced
on the Cross.

The message is rooted in the Gospel

10. The appeal of the Lady of the message of Fatima is so deeply rooted in the Gospel and the whole
of Tradition that the Church feels that the message imposes a commitment on her. She has responded
through the Servant of God, Pius XII, (whose episcopal ordination took place precisely on May 13, 1917).
He consecrated the human race and especially the
peoples of Russia to the Immaculate Heart of Mary.
Was not that consecration his response to the evangelical eloquence of the call of Fatima?

In its Dogmatic Constitution on the Church *(Lu-
men Gentium)* and its Pastoral Constitution on the
Church in the Modern World *(Gaudium et Spes)*, the
Second Vatican Council amply illustrated the reasons
for the link between the Church and the world of today. Furthermore, its teaching on Mary's special place
in the mystery of Christ and the Church, bore mature
fruit in Paul VI's action in calling Mary "Mother of the
Church," and thus indicating more profoundly the nature of her union with the Church and of her care for
the world, for mankind, for each human being, and
for all the nations. What characterizes them is her
motherhood.

This brought a further deepening of understanding of the meaning of the act of consecrating that the Church is called upon to perform with the help of the Heart of Christ's Mother and ours.

The denial of God

11. Today John Paul II, successor of Peter, continuer of the work of Pius, John and Paul, and particular heir of the Second Vatican Council, presents himself before the Mother of the Son of God in her shrine at Fatima. In what way does he come? He presents himself, reading again with trepidation the motherly call to penance, to conversion, the ardent appeal of the Heart of Mary that resounded at Fatima sixty-five years ago. Yes, he reads it again with trepidation in his heart, because he sees how many people and societies—how many Christians—have gone in the opposite direction to the one indicated in the message of Fatima. Sin has thus made itself firmly at home in the world, and denial of God has become widespread in the ideologies, ideas and plans of human beings.

But for this very reason the evangelical call to repentance and conversion, uttered in the Mother's message, remains ever relevant. It is still more relevant than it was sixty-five years ago. It is still more urgent. And so it is to be the subject of next year's Synod of Bishops, for which we are already preparing.

The successor of Peter presents himself here also as a witness to the immensity of human suffering, a witness to the almost apocalyptic menaces looming over the nations and mankind as a whole. He is trying to embrace these sufferings with his own weak human heart, as he places himself before the mystery of the heart of the Mother, the Immaculate Heart of Mary.

In the name of these sufferings and with awareness of the evil that is spreading throughout the world and menacing the individual human being, the nations, and mankind as a whole, Peter's successor presents himself here with greater faith in the redemption of the world, in the saving Love that is always stronger, always more powerful than any evil. My heart is oppressed when I see the sin of the world and the whole range of menaces gathering like a dark cloud over mankind, but it also rejoices with hope as I once more do what has been done by my predecessors, when they consecrated the world to the heart of the Mother, when they consecrated especially to that heart those peoples which particularly need to be consecrated. Doing this means consecrating the world to Him who is infinite Holiness. This Holiness means redemption. It means a love more powerful than evil. No "sin of the world" can ever overcome this Love.

Once more this act is being done. Mary's appeal is not for just once. Her appeal must be taken up by generation after generation, in accordance with the ever new "signs of the times." It must be unceasingly returned to. It must ever be taken up anew.

The faith of the Church

12. The author of the Apocalypse wrote: "And I saw the holy city, the new Jerusalem, coming down out of heaven from God, prepared as a bride adorned for her husband; and I heard a loud voice from the throne saying, 'Behold, the dwelling of God is with men. He will dwell with them, and they shall be his people, and God himself will be with them'" (Rev. 21: 2-3). This is the faith by which the Church lives. This is the faith with which the people of God make their journey. "The dwelling of God is with men" on earth even now.

In that dwelling is the heart of the Bride and Mother, Mary, a heart adorned with the jewel of her Immaculate Conception. The heart of the Bride and Mother which was opened beneath the Cross by the word of her Son to a great new love for man and the world. The heart of the Bride and Mother which is aware of all the sufferings of individuals and societies on earth.

The people of God are pilgrims along the ways of this world in an eschatological direction. They are making their pilgrimage towards the eternal Jerusalem, towards "the dwelling of God with men." God will there "wipe away every tear from their eyes, and death shall be no more, neither shall there be mourning nor crying nor pain any more, for the former things have passed away."

But at present "the former things" are still in existence. They constitute the temporary setting of our pilgrimage. For that reason we look towards "Him who sits upon the throne and says, 'Behold, I make all things new'" (Rev.21:5). And together with the Evangelist and Apostle, we try to see with the eyes of faith "the new heaven and the new earth"; for the first heaven and the first earth have passed away.

But "the first heaven and the first earth" still exist about us and within us. We cannot ignore them. But this enables us to recognize what an immense grace was granted to us human beings when, in the midst of our pilgrimage, there shone forth on the horizon of the faith of our times this "great portent, a woman" (Rev. 12:1).

Yes, truly we can repeat: "O daughter, you are blessed by the Most High God above all women on earth...walking in the straight path before our God... you have avenged our ruin."

Truly, indeed, you are blessed.

Yes, here and throughout the Church, in the heart of every individual and in the world as a whole, may you be blessed, O Mary, our sweet Mother.

APPENDIX IV

ACT OF CONSECRATION OF POPE JOHN PAUL II AT ST. PETER'S BASILICA, ROME, MARCH 25, 1984

"WE HAVE RECOURSE to your protection, holy Mother of God." As we utter the words of this antiphon with which the Church of Christ has prayed for centuries, we find ourselves today before you, Mother, in the Jubilee Year of the Redemption.

We find ourselves united with all the Pastors of the Church in a particular bond whereby we constitute a body and a college, just as by Christ's wish the Apostles constituted a body and college with Peter. In the bond of this union, we utter the words of the present Act, in which we wish to include, once more, the Church's hopes and anxieties for the modern world.

Forty years ago and again ten years later, your servant Pope Pius XII, having before his eyes the painful experiences of the human family, entrusted and consecrated to your Immaculate Heart the whole world, especially the peoples for which by reason of their situation you have particular love and solicitude. This world of individuals and nations we too have before our eyes today; the world of the second millennium that is drawing to a close, the modern world, our world!

The Church, mindful of the Lord's words: "Go . . . and make disciples of all nations . . . and lo, I am with you always, to the close of the age" (Matt. 28:19–20), has, at the Second Vatican Council, given fresh life to her awareness of her mission in this world.

And therefore, O Mother of individuals and peoples, you who know all their sufferings and their hopes, you who have a mother's awareness of all the struggles between good and evil, between light and darkness, which afflict the modern world, accept the cry which we, moved by the Holy Spirit, address directly to your Heart. Embrace, with the love of the Mother and Handmaid of the Lord, this human world of ours, which we entrust and consecrate to you, for we are full of concern for the earthly and eternal destiny of individuals and peoples.

In a special way we entrust and consecrate to you those individuals and nations which particularly need to be thus entrusted and consecrated.

We have recourse to your protection, holy Mother of God: despise not our petitions in our necessities.

Behold, as we stand before you, Mother of Christ, before your Immaculate Heart, we desire, together with the whole Church, to unite ourselves with the consecration which, for love of us, your Son made of

Himself to the Father: "For their sake, He said, "I consecrate myself that they also may be consecrated in the truth" (Jn. 17:19). We wish to unite ourselves with our Redeemer in this, His consecration for the human race, which, in His divine Heart, has the power to obtain pardon and to secure reparation.

The power of this consecration lasts for all time and embraces all individuals, peoples and nations. It overcomes every evil that the spirit of darkness is able to awaken, and has in fact awakened in our times, in the heart of man and in his history.

How deeply we feel the need for the consecration of humanity and the world—our modern world—in union with Christ Himself! For the redeeming work of Christ must be shared in by the world through the Church. The present Year of the Redemption shows this: the special Jubilee of the whole Church.

Above all creatures, may you be blessed, you, the Handmaid of the Lord, who in the fullest way obeyed the divine call! Hail to you, who are wholly united to the redeeming consecration of your Son! Mother of the Church! Enlighten the people of God along the paths of faith, hope and love! Help us to live in the truth of the consecration of Christ for the entire human family of the modern world.

In entrusting to you, O Mother, the world, all individuals and peoples, we also entrust to you this very consecration of the world, placing it in your motherly heart.

Immaculate Heart! Help us to conquer the menace of evil, which so easily takes root in the hearts of the people of today, and whose immeasurable effects already weigh down upon our modern world and seem to block the paths towards the future!

From famine and war, deliver us.

From nuclear war, from incalculable self-destruction, from every kind of war, deliver us.

From sins against the life of man from its very beginning, deliver us.

From hatred and from the demeaning of the dignity of the children of God, deliver us.

From every kind of injustice in the life of society, both national and international, deliver us.

From readiness to trample on the commandments of God, deliver us.

From attempts to stifle in human hearts the very truth of God, deliver us.

From the loss of awareness of good and evil, deliver us.

From sins against the Holy Spirit, deliver us, deliver us.

Accept, O Mother of Christ, this cry laden with the sufferings of all individual human beings, laden with the sufferings of whole societies.

Help us with the power of the Holy Spirit to conquer all sin: individual sin and the "sin of the world," sin in all its manifestations.

Let there be revealed, once more in the history of the world, the infinite saving power of the Redemption: the power of merciful Love! May it put a stop to evil! May it transform consciences! May your Immaculate Heart reveal for all the light of Hope!

APPENDIX V

ACT OF ENTRUSTMENT TO THE MOTHER OF GOD OF POPE JOHN PAUL II AT FATIMA, MAY 13, 1991

1. "Holy Mother of the Redeemer,

Gate of Heaven, Star of the Sea, help your people who want to rise again." Once again we turn to you, Mother of Christ and of the Church, gathered at your feet in Cova da Iria, to thank you for what you have done in these difficult years for the Church, for each of us, and for all humanity.

2. "Monstra te esse matrem!"

How many times we have invoked you! And today we are here to thank you because you have always listened to us. You showed yourself a mother: Mother of the Church, a missionary on this earth's roads towards the awaited third Christian millennium; Mother of all people by your constant protection which sheltered us from disaster and irreparable destruction, and promoted progress and modern social conquests; Mother of the nations by the unexpected changes which restored confidence to peoples who were oppressed and humiliated for so long; Mother of life, by the many signs with which you have accompanied us, defending us from evil and the power of death; My Mother for ever, and especially on May 13, 1981, when I felt your helpful presence at my side; Mother of every person who fights for life which does not die; Mother of the humanity redeemed by the blood of Christ; Mother of perfect love, of hope and peace; Holy Mother of the Redeemer.

3. "Monstra te esse Matrem!"

Yes, continue to show yourself a mother to everyone, because the world needs you. The new conditions of peoples and the Church are still precarious and unstable. There is the danger of replacing Marxism with another form of atheism which, praising freedom, tends to destroy the roots of human and Christian morality.

Mother of hope, walk with us! Walk with the men and women along this last furrow of the twentieth century, with the people of every race and culture, of every age and condition. Walk with the people toward solidarity and love, walk with our young people, the craftsmen of future days of peace.

There is need for you in the nations which recently acquired room for freedom and are now committed to building their future. There is need for you in Europe which, from East to West, cannot reclaim its true identity without discovering its common Christian roots. There is need for you in the world to resolve the many violent conflicts which still threaten it.

4. "Monstra te esse Matrem!"

Show yourself the Mother of the poor, of those who are dying of hunger and illness, of those who are suffering from torture and others' abuse of power, of those who cannot find a job, a home or refuge, of those who are oppressed and exploited, of those who are without hope, or who in vain seek quiet far from God. Help us to defend life, a reflection of divine life, help us to defend it always, from its dawn to its natural end.

Show yourself a Mother of unity and peace. Stop violence and injustice everywhere, help harmony and unity grow in families and respect and understanding among peoples. May peace, true peace, reign on earth! Mary, give the world Christ, our peace. May peoples not dig anew the pits of hatred and revenge; may the world not yield to the desire for a false well-being which harms the dignity of the person and endangers forever the resources of Creation.

Show yourself the Mother of hope! Watch over the road which still awaits us. Watch over the people and the new situations of peoples still menaced by the threat of war. Watch over the leaders of nations and those who influence the fate of humanity. Watch over the Church which is always threatened by the spirit of the world. Especially watch over the coming Special Assembly of the Synod of Bishops, an important phase in the path of the new evangelization of Europe. Watch over my Petrine ministry in the service of the Gospel and the human person towards the new goals of the Church's missionary activity.

Totus tuus!

5. In collegial unity with the Pastors, in communion with the entire People of God spread to the four corners of the earth, today I renew the filial entrustment of the human race to you. With confidence we entrust everyone to you. With you we want to follow Christ, Redeemer of mankind. May weariness not overburden us, nor hard work slow us down; may difficulties not extinguish our courage nor sadness the joy of our heart.

Mary, Mother of the Redeemer, continue to show yourself Mother of all and watch over our path. May we joyfully see your Son in heaven. Amen!

PICTURE CREDITS

Augustine Publishing Company: page 14.
Bishop Pavol Hnilica, SJ: page 139.
Marian Helpers Bulletin, Stockbridge, MA 01263:
page 51.
Sanctuary of Fatima: Frontispiece; pages 81, 114,
and 180.
*Vice-Postulation Center for Francisco and Jacinta
Marto, Fatima:* page 26.

SOURCES

The following publications have been quoted in
this book and are recommended to readers for further
information:

Fatima Family Messenger, Subscription Depart-
ment, New Hope, KY 40052 USA.
Soul Magazine, World Apostolate of Fatima,
Washington, NJ 07882. In Britain: 36 Bowood Road,
Swindon, Wiltshire, SN1 4LP.